John Patterson MacLean

First Annual Gathering of the Clan MacLean Association of

North America

John Patterson MacLean

First Annual Gathering of the Clan MacLean Association of North America

ISBN/EAN: 9783337389499

Printed in Europe, USA, Canada, Australia, Japan

Cover: Foto ©Suzi / pixelio.de

More available books at **www.hansebooks.com**

FIRST ANNUAL GATHERING

OF THE

CLAN MACLEAN ASSOCIATION

OF

NORTH AMERICA,

HELD IN THE CITY OF CHICAGO, JUNE 12-16, 1893.

PREPARED AND EDITED
BY
J. P. MacLEAN.

ST. JOHN, N. B.:
TELEGRAPH BOOK AND JOB PRINT, CANTERBURY STREET.
1893.

MACLEAN TABLE.

COAT OF ARMS. — "Sir Hector MacLean, Chief of the MacLeans, an ancient loyal, potent clan, in the Highlands of Scotland, of which there have been many brave men. The achievement of the Family of MacLean, as illuminated in the Book of James Espline, Marchmont Herald, 1630, has four coats quarterly: 1st, Argent, a rock gules; 2nd, Argent, a dexter hand fesse, ways couped gules. holding a cross, crosslet fitched in pale azure; 3rd, A lymphad sable; 4th, Argent, a salmon niant proper, and in chief, two eagles' heads waged affronted gules. Crest: A tower embattled argent. Motto: Virtue Mine Honor. Which achievement is represented standing on a compartment representing green sand and sea — out of the last issueth two selches proper for supporters."

CREST—A battle-axe between a laurel and cypress branch. Motto above the crest: Altera Merces — another offering.

BADGE — Crowberry.

WAR CRY — Bas na beatha — Death or Life. *March* — Caismeachd Echuinn mhic Ailein nan sop — Warning of Hector, son of Allan of the Wisp of Straw.

CLAN GATHERING — Ceann na Drochaide Bige — Head of the little bridge.

LAMENT — An Ribein Gorm — Blue ribbon.

ADVERTISEMENT.

After the gathering of the MacLeans in Chicago, there was a general feeling that a complete report of the proceedings should be published. To leave the matter for the consideration of the next session in Toronto was thought to be inexpedient, although it is sincerely hoped that said meeting will take such action as will be satisfactory to all the members of the Association. With a view to preserve the records, and to present the same in a permanent form, I have taken the responsibility of editing and publishing the same. I submit my work to the favorable consideration of the members of the Clan.

J. P. MACLEAN.

July 27th, 1893.

SIR FITZROY DONALD MacLEAN, BART.

LADY MacLean.

CLAN MACLEAN ASSOCIATION

OF

NORTH AMERICA.

I — NARRATIVE.

On January 29th, 1893, I wrote a letter to Arthur
A. MacLean, President Cairo Lumber Company, stating
if he would tender the use of his office, I would notify
all the MacLeans in the City of Chicago to meet me
there on January 17th, in order to take action relative
to inviting Colonel Sir Fitzroy Donald MacLean, Bart.,
Chief of the Clan, to visit the World's Columbian
Exposition, and during his stay to be the guest of
his Clansmen. Mr. MacLean responded immediately
to the message, in which he not only offered the use
of his office, but warmly seconded the proposition.
Having a list of eighty of the name, residents of
Chicago, I notified all to meet me in the office of
Arthur A. MacLean, The Rookery, at 12 M., on Jan'y
17th. At the same time I caused notices to be inserted
in the daily papers of Chicago.

At the appointed time, the private office of Mr.
MacLean was filled with descendants of Gillean, most
of whom were strangers to each other. On my own

motion, Archibald MacLean, Esq., of Rockford, Ill.,
was made temporary chairman. On assuming the
chair, Mr. MacLean stated that the object of the meeting was fully known to all. He then proceeded to
give his reasons why the Chief and all the Chieftains
should be invited to the World's Fair, and to be the
guests of the Clansmen during their stay. George
C. McLean, of Janesville, Wis., vigorously seconded
the remarks offered by the chairman. On a vote
being taken, it was unanimously carried that the Chief
and Chieftains of the Clan be invited to Chicago, and
that the Chief should name the time. The meeting
then elected W. A. McLean Permanent President; S.
P. MacLean, Secretary; J. P. MacLean, Cor. Secretary,
and A. A. MacLean, Treasurer. The Corresponding
Secretary was directed to communicate the desire of
the meeting to the Chief, and report the result to the
President. The meeting then adjourned, to meet at
the call of the President.

Before leaving Chicago, on that day, I addressed a
letter to the Chief, conveying to him the sense of the
meeting, requesting his acceptance, and for him to
name the time that would be most convenient for him
to attend the World's Fair, and inviting him to be the
guest of his Clansmen.

The action thus taken was reported to the Associated Press, and the next day appeared in the leading
papers of America.

February 16th, the Chief's letter of acceptance was
received, the following being a copy : —

THE LEES, FOLKNSTONE, KENT, ENG.,
February 4th, 1893.

PROFESSOR J. P. MACLEAN,
Corresponding Secretary,

MY DEAR SIR:

Nothing in this universe could have touched my heart to the extent of the message just received from my Clansmen on the other side of the Atlantic.

I at once accept their courteous invitation to become their guest, and Lady MacLean will gladly accompany me to Chicago to visit the Columbian Exposition — if it pleases the Great Director of all events to give us health and strength to do it.

Pray convey to those gentlemen who were present at the meeting held on January 17th, my high sense of their loyalty to their Ancient Family Traditions and to their Chief, who once more repeats the oath made by his ancestors before starting on an expedition — as far back as the 11th century : —

> " The heavens are above us,
>   The land below us,
> The ocean around us,
>   Everything in a circle about us ;
> If the heavens do not fall,
>   Casting from their high fortresses
> The stars like rain on the face of the earth ;
>   If shocks from within
> Do not shatter the land itself ;
>   If the ocean from its blue solitude
>   Does not rise up over
> The brows of all living things " —

I will meet my Clansmen in Chicago.

Believe me,
Yours ever faithfully,

FITZROY DONALD MACLEAN, BART.,
of Dowart, Brolas and Morvern,
Chief of the Clan.

In a postscript the Chief added that he would sail from Liverpool on the S. S. "Majestic," Wednesday, May 31st.

The same day on which the above was received, I communicated its contents to the President, and also notified the Secretary and Treasurer.

The President called a meeting to be held at 2 p. m. of March 1st, in the office of the Treasurer, and wrote to me urgently to be present. During this session the whole question was gone over, the financial part receiving the greater consideration. The meeting fully realized that there was hard and persistent labor before each member. It was desired to reach every member of the Clan in North America, and every one to have a special invitation, regardless of the method of spelling the name. An effort should be made to quicken the Clan spirit in every one. It was understood that there were innumerable families that had been resident in the New World so long that they had lost all trace of their ancestry ; others had neglected such opportunities as had been afforded them, while still others were indifferent. It was decided that circulars should be sent to every one of the name whose address could be obtained. Anticipating this, I had prepared a draft, and submitted it to the meeting. The Chief's letter of acceptance was read at the opening of the session, and was received with prolonged applause. Committees on Finance, Arrangements and Reception were appointed. Also an Advisory one. The Corresponding Secretary was directed to have a circular printed, and to send one to every one of the name on his list—having reported that he had about 3,000 names—and to draw on the Treasurer for funds. A call for contributions was now made, when nearly every one contributed five dollars each. It was also decided that the week beginning June 12th should be one of festivities, during which time there should be a Reception and Banquet.

The draft of the circular submitted I revised, and on March 8th I commenced to send it through the mails, the following being a copy:

HAIL TO THE CHIEF!

The Fiery Cross has not been sent over the mountains or hills of Mull, Morvern, Coll, Tiree or Islay, summoning the MacLeans to respond to the call of their Chief, since 1745, nor has their slogan — *Bas na Beatha* — been heard. The plaided warriors of MacLean sleep in their Island graves.

By these Presents all the MacLeans, and those related by direct descent or married into the Clan, especially those residing in the United States and Canada, are summoned to assemble in the City of Chicago, during the week commencing June the 12th, 1893, to welcome the Hereditary Chief of The Ancient and Great Clan MacLean, Colonel Sir Fitzroy Donald MacLean, Bart., who has positively promised to be present, and will leave Liverpool on the S.S. "Majestic," Wednesday, May 31st, and will be the guest of the MacLeans of North America, at the World's Columbian Exposition.

The following Chieftains of the Clan have also been invited to be present: Captain Murdoch Gillian Maclaine of Lochbuie, Archibald John Maclean of Pennycross, Alex. John Hew Maclean of Ardgour, The Maclean of Coll, Robert Cutler McLean of Kingerloch.

A reception and banquet will be given during the week —

the exact time not yet determined — at which there will be
toasts, responses and songs, bagpipe and other music.

The committee suggests that all — ladies and gentlemen
— should wear the MacLean dress Tartan.

Please observe the following directions : —

1. All who will be present, and will also attend the
banquet, are requested, at as early a date as possible, to
notify S. P. Maclean, reporter, " The Tribune," Chicago.

2. All desiring the dress Tartan can secure as many
yards as wanted, at $1 per yard ; Sashes — which have been
suggested — three yards long, exclusive of the fringe — at
$3 each, all made out of Scotch wool of the finest texture,
and most durable colors. To secure the Tartan, money
must be sent as early as possible to J. P. MacLean, Mor-
rison, Ill. If goods are to be sent by mail, postage must be
added at the rate of nine cents to the yard.

Let all help make this a great occasion. Remember, this
is the only instance of a Highland Chief having been
invited to this country by his Clansmen. Let all unite to
renew the Ancient Ties of Clanship.

As the committee has not the address of all our Clansmen,
it is hoped that every one will feel it to be their duty to
invite all they may know to participate on this occasion,
which is destined to be historical.

W. A. McLEAN, *President,*   S. P. MACLEAN, *Rec. Sec'y,*
    4001 Grand Boulevard.   The Tribune Building.
A. A. MACLEAN, *Treasurer,*   J. P. MACLEAN, *Cor. Sec'y,*
    541 The Rookery.   Morrison, Ill.

COMMITTEES.

Advisory — W. A. McLean, S. P. Maclean, J. P. Mac-
Lean.

Finance — James A. McLane, 100 Washington Street ;
W. C. McClaine, 4259 Cottage Grove Avenue ; Charles

McLean, 124 31st Street; A. B. McLean, Jr., 152 LaSalle Street.

Arrangements — Thomas A. Maclean, 541 The Rookery; J. W. McLean, 44 State Street; Archibald Maclean, Rockford, Illinois.

Reception — Capt. A. B. McLean, Sr., 110 Fifth Avenue; A. A. Maclean, 541 The Rookery; Colin C. McLean, Janesville, Wis. ; W. D. McLain, 200 Oakwood Boulevard.

Chicago, Ill., March 8th, 1893.

With this, on a separate sheet, I sent a copy of the Chief's letter of acceptance.

On March 2nd, I sent letters of invitation to The MacLean of Pennycross and The Maclaine of Lochbuie, followed on the 6th by letters to The MacLean of Ardgour, The MacLean of Coll, The MacLean of Dochgarroch, and a few days later one to The MacLean of Kingerloch. The MacLean of Pennycross was the only Chieftain who was able to respond favorably.

After sending copies of the circulars to every name on my list in the United States and Ontario, I received a letter from the Treasurer, in which he directed me to turn over to him a list of all the names I possessed, and all the circulars on hand. Immediately I complied with the order, and at the same time reported what I had done. The order was a welcome one. For nearly three weeks I had been almost incessantly engaged in enclosing envelopes and mailing the circulars. I now devoted a portion of my time in inditing letters to such parties as I thought might take an interest in the coming gathering. I also made the attempt to organize by States and have some one in each Commonwealth to lead the movement.

About this time, W. B. Maclean and other Macleans in Toronto, Ont., became interested in the enterprise, and took hold in earnest. Circulars were furnished them for distribution, and a list of over 700 of the name in Canada.

As I still had full charge of the Tartan interest, I busied myself in urging all to secure a pattern.

The third and last meeting of the Association I attended was the evening of May 2nd. At this session quite a number of ladies were present. The question of their organizing an auxiliary branch, and what method of dress they should wear, were discussed. Also the prospective outlook was considered.

As the time drew near, I wrote a letter to George H. McLean, Esq., of New York, requesting him to look after the Chief on his arrival, and to show him such hospitality as should be given to the head of the Clan. Mr. McLean promptly replied that he would do all within his power to make everything pleasant during his stay in the City of New York. I also wrote to the Hon. Charles F. MacLean, to look after the interests of Chieftain MacLean of Pennycross. The reply was also cordial, and that the Chieftain would receive due hospitality.

The selection of W. A. McLean as President was very fortunate. He entered upon the work with all the enthusiasm of a youth, and devoted his entire time to the enterprise. His mind fairly teemed with plans and expedients. Besides mailing thousands of circulars, he wrote not less than five hundred letters; nor in all the labor given did he grow weary.

Arthur A. MacLean, possessing a cool judgment, was invaluable. He had the capacity to weigh every suggestion, and point out which was the best.

Thomas A. MacLean threw into the work all the fiery, sanguine enthusiasm of youth, and with his perpetual good nature, proved himself of great value. He was full of suggestions, with zeal sufficient to carry any one to completion. James A. McLane looked carefully into the financial part, and brought to bear his long experience as a business manager. There are others also deserving of special mention. Taken all together, those who engaged in the movement were as happy and as devoted a band as ever came together to promote a single enterprise. Their motto was: Success.

Words of encouragement were received from those not directly concerned in the undertaking. Early in the campaign I received a letter from Mr. S. A. McLean, of Bay City, Mich., in which he stated that he fully realized that funds were necessary to accomplish such an enterprise, and if necessary to draw on him for $25.00. If more was necessary, he would stand another assessment. It may be needless to remark that the Treasurer drew on him at once.

By the first of May, the local committee in Chicago had fully completed their arrangements, in consequence of which they felt authorized to issue the following circular: —

HEADQUARTERS CHICAGO ASSOCIATION CLAN MACLEAN,

THE ROOKERY,

Southeast Corner LaSalle and Adams Streets.

CHICAGO, ILL.

DEAR SIR AND CLANSMAN :

The final arrangements for the great gathering of the Clan in Chicago, commencing on Monday, June 12th, are now completed. The Chief, Sir Fitzroy Donald MacLean, Bart.; Count MacLean, Chieftain of the MacLeans of Sweden (who is also President of the MacLean's Association of Glasgow, Scotland, escorted by a delegation from that Association), and the Chieftains of Pennycross, Lochbuie, Ardgour, Urquhart, and Kingerloch are expected to arrive in Chicago on the 12th, and on the 13th a reception will be given at the Auditorium to these distinguished gentlemen and their families by the Clan MacLean in America, as represented on that occasion.

On the 15th, a Grand Banquet will be given in their honor by the Association at the Auditorium, which, we already have the assurance, will be largely attended. Toasts and sentiments appropriate to the occasion will be proposed and responded to by representative men of the Clan from different States, and from the British Provinces. The price of banquet tickets is $5.00. It is especially desired that the ladies shall attend the banquet as well as all the other entertainments of the gathering.

On the evening of the 16th a MacLean Concert will be given at Central Music Hall, by members of the Clan, assisted by the Highland Association of Illinois; the music at this concert will be of a high class, and exclusively Scottish, both vocal and instrumental; the vocal part consisting of Highland songs in both the ancient Gaelic and the English; there will be a variety of the Scottish national dances; the instrumental music will be also strictly Scottish, and will be rendered by a magnificent orchestra and a band of Highland pipers. The solo numbers will be by eminent Scottish singers, and the chorus a large and thoroughly trained one. This concert will be a great musical event of the Exposition year, and will add materially in making memorable this great gathering of the Clan. The Chief, Chieftains and their families, with other distinguished guests, will be present at this concert. We have already letters from nearly every State in the Union, from various places in Ontario and the other Provinces of the Dominion of Canada, and also from MacLeans in Holland, which place beyond all doubt the magnificent success of this, the first gathering of a Highland Clan in America, and the unique and memorable fact that it is inviting, as it did of old, not their chosen "Prince Charlie" to come over the stream, but their honored Chief and Chieftains to come over the broad ocean to receive the hospitalities of their Clansmen in the New World.

A special train of MacLeans from Toronto, accompanied by the Pipers' Band of the 48th Highlanders, will attend the gathering, and this, we believe, will be only the "advance guard" of the MacLeans from other parts of the Dominion who will attend; from each of the States there will be large delegations coming in organized bodies, so that we may confidently say that we have every reason to expect a gathering which will be recalled and remembered by all who are so fortunate as to participate in it, and will be a marked event which our children will often refer to with pride after we are gone.

The fee for membership in this Association is, for residents of Chicago, $5.00, and for non-residents, $2.50. The payment of this fee is required from each member on enrolling

2

his name, and entitles him to all the privileges of membership, among which is, admission to the reception for himself
and the female members and minor boys of his family (which
admission will be by ticket only, and which will be furnished
to each member on payment of the fee), and will also entitle
him to have his name appear in the History of the Gathering, which will be published in pamphlet form and furnished
to members only. Non-resident members will be given all
desired information by the officers and committees of this
Association, who will gladly do all in their power to make
the visit of our Clansmen to the World's Fair City a pleasant
and memorable one.

Those desiring to join this Association (and all MacLeans,
without regard to the manner of spelling their name, are
heartily invited to join it), should address without delay,
Arthur A. MacLean, Treasurer, at Headquarters Clan Mac-
Lean, Rookery Building, Chicago, with remittance to cover
their membership fee, also signifying whether or not they
will attend the Banquet, and a membership ticket will be
sent them by return mail.

All MacLeans visiting this city are cordially invited to call
at Clan Headquarters, where they will be heartily welcomed.

ARTHUR A. MACLEAN,   W. A. McLEAN,
           Treasurer.   *President.*

P. S. — As an evidence of the intense interest that this
gathering is awakening, not among the MacLeans only, we
select from numerous similar ones, the following letter from
the Chieftain of a kindred Clan, which cannot fail to evoke
a responsive sentiment in the hearts of every MacLean :

AT THE MANNING HOUSE,

WINDSOR, ONT., CANADA, 12th April, 1893.

MY DEAR SIR :

In the behalf of the Macneil, Hereditary Chief of the Clan Neil of Barra, aged and infirm, sojourning in this country, I present compliments to all the gentlemen of the various committees, and beg to congratulate you, and them, on the unprecedented example the proud sons of Dowart have set to the Scots of America in calling their Clansmen together on the occasion of the Columbian Exposition, and tendering their worthy Chief a grand reception.

The spirit of the Macneil thrills at such an expression of fidelity to their *cean kinne* as those Macleans have given, and it moves him to exclaim, " Though our Clans are scattered to the four corners of the earth, and some of us dispossessed wanderers in many lands, yet our children have not forgotten us ! "

The heartfelt prayer of the Macneil and the son of the Macneil is, that Him who alone can support the oath of the Maclean will command the earth and the inhabitants, and all the elements to join in the propitiousness of this extraordinary and noble occasion.

Yours very sincerely,

AMBROSE MACNEIL,

Chieftain next of Kin.

To S. P. MACLEAN, Esq.,

Secretary;

Chicago.

That it became necessary for the local committee to put forth every effort within their power to make the gathering a success, is evident when the nature of the untoward circumstances which surrounded them is considered. The Columbian Exhibition was to be the greatest event in the history of Chicago. The people there expected the whole world would be on tiptoe, and that all the nations of the earth would come *en masse.* Consequently, all the people of the city were invited to pick the fatted goose. The leading hotels advertised exhorbitant rates, which led householders to charge accordingly ; the railways would make no concessions, and the Exposition was thrown open when scarcely a building was in readiness. These facts were seized upon by the newspapers of the country, which carefully saw that the *status* should lose nothing in the representation. Scattered all over the country were thousands of MacLeans, in moderate circumstances, who willingly would have come to Chicago had it not been for the fear of being fleeced. Whatever time might have been selected would necessarily interfere with the interests of some. On the whole, the time appointed was as favorable as any other, although the farmers were in the midst of their busy season. The only hold now possessed by the committee was to arouse Clan pride. It was beyond their power to lessen the prices determined on by railways, hotels and private citizens ; but they determined to assist the Clansmen in securing accommodations. However, undeterred, and fully believing in the success of the gathering, the following circular was put forth : —

HEADQUARTERS CHICAGO ASSOCIATION CLAN MACLEAN,

THE ROOKERY,

Southeast Corner LaSalle and Adams Streets.

CHICAGO, ILL., May 26th, 1893.

The Committee of Arrangements for the Banquet at the Auditorium, on June 15th, desire to reserve seats for all our Clansmen intending to be present, and to enable them to do so, they *must* be notified not later than June 6th.

Requests for seats from our Scottish friends (not Mac-Leans) have been very urgent, but up to the present have been in every case denied.

The Committee have decided that they cannot reserve seats beyond the above date (June 6th). Will you please ascertain the number of our Clansmen in your neighborhood who desire seats reserved, and kindly advise us, giving their names and address.

Should any desire hotel accommodations, the Committee will secure same for them on their being advised of the class desired. *Good* accommodations, on the "American plan," can be secured at from $3 to $5 per day, and *good* rooms, without board, at from $1.50 up, per person.

May we rely on your attention to this matter and *prompt* advice? It is of the greatest importance that we *know* how many of our Clansmen to provide for.

Yours very truly,

PRESIDENT.

II. — ARRIVAL IN NEW YORK.

Colonel Sir Fitzroy Donald MacLean, Bart., Chief of the Clan, sailed from Liverpool, on board the S.S. "Majestic," May 31st, and arrived in New York June 7th. At the steamer he was met by George H. McLean, Esq., who escorted him to his hotel, The Waldorf, where apartments had been previously secured. That evening he was the guest of Mr. McLean at the Manhatten Club. The next day he was taken out for a drive through the city and Central Park, and in the evening Mr. and Mrs. McLean gave him a dinner — there being present several of the prominent MacLeans of the city. On Friday the Chief was taken over the Riverside drive, by Washington Bridge, returning by Central Park. In the evening, a dinner was given him at Delmonico's, followed by a box at Palmer's

Theatre. On Saturday, escorted by a large party of MacLeans, the Chief took a trip up the Hudson to West Point, a place he had long desired to visit. The day was finished by a repast tendered by Mr. and Mrs. G. H. McLean. On Sunday, accompanied by Hon. Donald McLean and family, the Chief left New York for Chicago.

Archibald John Maclean, Esq., Chieftain of the Macleans of Pennycross, accompanied by Mrs. Maclean, left Liverpool on May 24th, and arrived in New York, per White Star Liner S.S. "Germanic," on June 2nd.

The "Germanic" was boarded at Staten Island by an officer sent by the Hon. Charles Fraser Maclean, who, on landing, escorted Pennycross and Mrs. Maclean to the Hoffman House Hotel. The Hon. Charles F. Maclean paid his respects in the afternoon.

Pennycross and Lady speak highly of the way they were entertained by the Clansmen.

They were taken a long drive through Central Park and the celebrated Riverside drive. There they were shown the Mosoleum of the late General Grant, in course of erection, as well as the temporary one where the remains are laying. They were also entertained at dinner by Hon. C. F. Maclean at his private residence, at which were also some of the Clansmen residing in the city.

Pennycross and Mrs. Maclean spent Sunday quietly, and in the afternoon went by elevated railroad to Greenwood Cemetery, Brooklyn, one of the finest cemetries in the world, where some of the family have their last resting place. Several days were spent visiting and receiving visits from friends, and going to places of amusement. Then, leaving New York *via* the Hudson River, by rail, a rest was made at Niagara to view the Falls. And Pennycross and Mrs. Maclean arrived at Chicago on June 10th. The President of the Clan Maclean received a dispatch in time to meet them at the depot, and accompanied the party to the Auditorium, where rooms had been secured for them.

III. — ARRIVAL IN CHICAGO.

When the train pulled up at the Michigan Central depot, in Chicago, on Monday, June 12th, on which were the Chief of MacLean and party, there stood on the platform a large delegation of prominent MacLeans, many of whom had recently arrived in the city. When the Chief stepped from the train, he was welcomed to the United States by President W. A. McLean, who introduced him to the rest of the delegation. After the greetings were over, the Chief took the arm of the President and started towards the entrance of the station, preceded by four pipers of the 48th Highlanders (Canadian), who were dressed in the Gordon plaid. The party took carriages, and drove to the Auditorium, where apartments had been secured.

IV. — RECEPTION.

All day Monday and Tuesday forenoon of June 12th and 13th, the Clansmen poured into the "Headquarters of the Clan MacLean Association," in The

Rookery building, where all received a hearty welcome, and where also pleasant acquaintances were
formed. Nearly all registered in the Visitors' Book.
The Reception was appointed for 3 o'clock p. m.,
June 13th, in the parlors of the Auditorium, but long
before that time the Clansmen, with their families,
filled the capacious rooms which had been assigned to
them. Every one wore the tartan in one form or
another. Some were dressed in the full Highland costume. Both the dress and hunting tartan was used.
One lady's dress was wholly of the hunting tartan.
Others wore ribbons, or scarfs in wool or silk. Shortly
after the appointed hour the shrill notes of the bagpipes were heard, and soon the stalwart forms of the
bagpipers entered the room, immediately followed the
Chief on the arm of the President, with the MacLean
of Pennycross and wife at their side. The Chief was
dressed in Highland costume, the plaid being the Mac-
Lean dress tartan. He carried his bonnet, with the
three eagles' feathers, in his right hand. He also wore
the Crimean medal, the two clasps, and the Turkish
war medal, which he had received for gallant and meri-
torious conduct in the Crimean war.

The MacLean of Pennycross was also dressed in full
Highland costume, composed of the MacLean dress
tartan. The claymore he wore belonged to his uncle
Charles, who was Junior Ensign in the 79th Cameron
Highlanders when they entered the field of Waterloo,
and who carried the colors unsullied on that eventful day. He was one of the two surviving officers,
although wounded. The dirk was worn at Culloden

CHIEFTAIN MacLEAN OF PENNYCROSS.

by one of his ancesters, and is the only known specimen of the same design and pattern. The Queen Mary brooch, worn in the kilt, has been handed down from father to son for many generations, as also the other two silver brooches, worn in kilt and plaid. The silver pistols are very handsome specimens of old MacLean flintlock weapons; perhaps nothing handsomer of the kind is in existence. The engraving is very chaste. The old cairn gorm buttons, in quaint old silver setting, are unique, and were greatly admired. The kilt ornaments are composed entirely of valuable old family relics, worn by his ancestors.

The party formed in a semi-circle, with the pipers to their left, and the clansmen on every side. After the music had ceased, the President stepped out a little, and then, facing the Chief, welcomed him in behalf of the Association, declaring the great pleasure afforded to all in his acceptance of the invitation to come to America. It was not asking Prince Charlie to come over the stream and dine with MacLean, but asking MacLean to come over the ocean and partake of the hospitality of his kinsmen in the New World; that the message sent was one of peace, and it was a great gratification to the Clansmen to greet him. Turning to MacLean of Pennycross, the President welcomed him in well-chosen words, and then both were formally introduced to the assemblage.

The Chief, in responding, said : —

Mr. McLean, Clansmen, Ladies and Gentlemen:

I thank you most heartily, on my own part and for the gentleman of my Clan accompanying me, for this great

reception which you have accorded us, and for the kind
expressions you have made use of in your address.

We are very glad to have been able to avail ourselves
of the courteous invitation you were good enough to send
us "to visit the World's Columbian Exposition," and I
need hardly say how sensible we are of the compliment you
have paid us by assembling here in such numbers, so as to
give a real Highland welcome to the Chief of the Clan and
the heads of the leading houses.

As you are aware, I have only been here a few hours.
After receiving great hospitality at New York, I was
escorted by most courteous and agreeable members of the
Clan to this city, arriving here a stranger to you all, and
4,000 miles from my own home; but at the station before
the train reached Chicago, a deputation of distinguished
MacLeans (all veteran soldiers who had fought and bled for
their country, and held high appointments in the American
army) came to welcome me, grasped me by the hand, and
soon gained the object they had in view, viz., " To make me
feel at home before I was many moments in their society."

Mr. McLean, as President of the Association of MacLeans
formed in this city, I thank you for your kindness and
hospitality, and I thank you, ladies and gentlemen, for the
warm-hearted reception you have given us.   It is very
evident that the history and deeds of our ancesters are
treasured up by you all, and are not likely to be forgotten.

I trust that the honored name we bear will ever be upheld,
and that the future generations may illustrate by their life
and conduct, in whatever part of the world their destiny
may lead them, that the Clan is capable of maintaining its
ancient "prestige" in the nineteenth century.   Let the
name "MacLean" be your passport among all nations; let
it be recognized all over the world that he who owns it is

not only brave in battle, but upright and honest in all his actions, and one in whom implicit trust and confidence can be placed.

I make this charge especially to my younger Clansmen, for your Chief may never have another opportunity of doing so, and it is for you to inspire future generations with that respect and love for your race which is so deeply rooted in the hearts of all those whom I have the honor of addressing.

It is very gratifying to me to have the pleasure of meeting my Clansmen in America and Canada. I am aware that many of you have travelled several thousand miles to welcome your Chief (from Texas, California, San Francisco, Newfoundland, etc.). Such devotion has, I assure you, touched my heart in a manner which no words can express, and the good feeling you have displayed towards me and the gentleman of the Clan who has accompanied me will be recognized and appreciated by MacLeans, not only in Scotland, but all over the World.

I thank you once more for the great reception you have given us, and I trust that during my sojourn here, in this fair city, I may have many opportunities of meeting and conversing with you, and I deeply regret that my engagements in the "Old Country" oblige me to limit my visit to a few days only, for I would gladly remain longer amongst you.

After the reception was over an interesting interview took place between the Chief and an old soldier who had formerly served under his command in the 13th Hussars, who had travelled a long distance to see him, and had waited four hours for an opportunity of speaking to him.

MacLean of Pennycross responded in Gaelic, to the following purport: Neither in Gaelic nor English can

I express myself sufficiently well to enable me to tell
what is within my heart on this great occasion. Such
a gathering of the Clan from distant parts I never saw
before. Gaelic was the first language I ever spoke.
When I asked, as a child, for milk, it was in Gaelic;
and if the milk of human kindness has not been
dispensed to us ever since we set foot on American
soil, there is no such thing in the world as kindness;
it must go by a higher name. On behalf of my wife
and self I desire to thank you, and when I go home I
will tell the tale. One hundred thousand blessings on
you, and may you live long and smoke out of your
house.

Every Clansman present was then presented separ-
ately to the Chief, Chieftain and Mrs. Pennycross.

In the evening the guests were taken, in carriages,
to the World's Fair, that they might see the buildings
lighted by electricity.

V. — RE-UNION.

The headquarters of the Association were kept open
every day, that the Clansmen might have resting
place, and also to become better acquainted with one
another. Nearly all availed themselves of the opportunity. All day Wednesday the rooms were thronged
with members of the Clan. Here letters and telegrams
were received and dispatched, and such business trans-
acted as was deemed necessary. The genial Thomas
A. and amiable Arthur A. were ever present, and
anxious to do all in their power for the visiting Mac-
Leans.

On the afternoon of the 14th, the guests were driven about the city, and also taken to the Exposition. In the evening, boxes having been previously secured, they were taken to the Auditorium Theater, to witness the spectacular performance entitled, " America."

VI. — THE BANQUET.

During the greater part of Thursday, the 15th, the Clansmen poured in and out of headquarters, some staying but for a few minutes, and others remaining for social conversation. The guests were driven about the city in carriages, and also taken to the Columbian Exposition. But the special feature of this date was the banquet, which had been set to take place in the banqueting hall of the Auditorium, commencing at 8 o'clock p. m. The Clansmen filed into the room and took the seats assigned to them, a little after the appointed time. Every available seat was occupied. The Chief and Chieftain were dressed in Highland costume, the same as at the reception. Others were also noticed in full Highland costume. Most of the gentlemen wore a heavy MacLean dress tartan, in the form of a scarf, fastened to the shoulder by a brooch. Some of the ladies wore a silk scarf, and others ribbons. All had a MacLean insignia of the dress tartan. The guests and speakers — all accompanied by ladies — sat at the principal table, which faced the rest of the party. The bagpipes and the harpers sat in the gallery. The guests filed into the room to the music of the bagpipe. After all had been seated, the Divine blessing was invoked by Rev. Calvin B. McLean.

By the side of each plate was a handsomely printed
program for the evening, and designed as a souvenir.
The *menu* consisted of Scotch broth à l'Avon; white
fish "Dowart"; roast filet, Jardiniere; haggis à l'Ecos-
saise; punch Romaine; snipe on toast; lettuce salad;
pudding imperial; fancy ices; cake; French coffee;
topaz sherry; sauterne and champaign.

At intervals, there was music from the bagpipes
and the harpers' band. When the waiters brought in
the haggis, they were preceded by the chief piper.
When the French coffee had been served, the chief
piper marched three times around the banquet hall,
playing Highland airs, and then brought up behind
the chair of the Chief of the Clan, who rendered the
custom of his ancestors on similar occasions — *i. e.,*
gave the piper a glass of whiskey.

OUR GUESTS,

PROPOSED BY W. A. McLEAN.

The time for the toasts having arrived, the President,
W. A. McLean, arose from his seat, and in proposing
the toast "Our Guests," in substance, said : From all
parts of the United States and Canada our Clansmen
have come to do honor to our distinguished guests.
They desire to meet and become acquainted with the
Chief and Chieftain of our Clan. We come in the
pride of our noble ancestors, and are proud of our
present Chief and the MacLean of Pennycross. To us
this is a happy occasion, and the memory of it we will
carry with us as long as we live. The only thing to
mar this enjoyable occasion is the absence of Lady

MacLean. I but speak the voice of this assemblage when I say that we all deeply regret the circumstances which detain her at home, and we all sincerely trust that she will be speedily restored from her present indisposition.

We can boast a long line of brave ancestors and Clansmen, who were ever true to their Chief. On the battlefield of Inverkeithing the Clansmen not only rallied around the young Chief of Duard, but eight of them interposed their bodies between that of their Chief and the missiles of the enemy, each one crying, "Another for Hector!" I verily believe that there is not one present but would do likewise, should the occasion require, for the present Chief of our Clan. We trust that your stay among us, so far, has been pleasant, and that it may so continue; and that you all may long be spared upon the earth.

In response to the toast, Colonel Sir Fitzroy Donald MacLean, Bart., Chief of the Clan, arose and said:

My Clansmen, Ladies and Gentlemen:

I wish I could find adequate words with which to express my thanks for your most kind and courteous invitation to visit the World's Fair. I am very much touched by the great reception you have accorded me as Chief of the Clan MacLean. I am informed that no such gathering has taken place in this country before.

I assure you that no credit is due me for leaving my home and travelling 4,000 miles, for the cry of the children of my tribe reached me; and as the Clan never deserted my ancestors, either in battle or in the hour of need, I have felt it a pleasure to respond to their call. On this occasion, history only in part repeats itself, for in other days the Fiery Cross was sent forth by the Chief from old Duard Castle, and the place of rendezvous was usually some secret or lonely spot on the hills or shores of Mull or Morvern. In those days supplies were scanty, but in this 19th century the Chief receives a peaceable message—an invitation to see the wonders of the World in a fair city, and in a land flowing with milk and honey. Now we behold the Fiery Cross has become an emblem of peace, and no longer the symbol of war. You have paid me a great compliment by attending here in such large numbers. The presence of ladies is very gratifying, and I cannot help observing that the proverbial beauty of the race is well maintained in this assembly.

It is all the more kind in the great attention shown me when I learned that many of you have come a long distance, have been put to great inconvenience and expense, in order to greet me. Permit me to say at this point that I cannot tell you how deeply Lady MacLean regretted her inability to undertake the voyage. She particularly desired me to express her great sorrow at not being allowed by her physician to accompany me.

The circumstances which brought me to the United States are unprecedented, and the compliment is still greater from the fact of my being personally unknown to you. I declare unhesitatingly that no invitation ever left the shores of this country written in such courteous terms, and no individual was ever more highly honored than the present Chief of MacLean. Times have changed since the MacLeans of Duard headed the Clan at Harlaw, Glenlivet, Inverkeithing, Killiecrankie, and other noted fields of honor. I am truly thankful I have not come to see your blood spilled ; but, after inspecting you with the eye of an old soldier, I am not to be deceived, for I behold a determined look in your countenances, combined with a true Highland expression, which tells me you would not be far behind your Chief if Inver-keithing or Culloden had to be fought over again. Should the MacLean battle-cry reach your ears, "Fear eil airson Eachainn," the laurel or cypress would soon be our reward. Well do I remember the stern and determined appearance of the 42nd Highlanders on the morning of the battle of Alma. I recognized in the commanding officer, Sir Duncan Cameron, the embodiment of deliberation and bravery, and capable of overcoming the greatest difficulties. I fully believe my Clansmen to be made of just as true steel. The history of our Clan is so well known and studied by you all that I will only say we are much indebted to one gentleman residing in America, whom we all know to be Professor J. P. MacLean, the historian of our Clan.

I have favorable reports from all over the world of Mac-Leans who have distinguished themselves — names from Sweden, Germany, Austria, Australia and India. In this country I find a body of intelligent men who, by their own exertions, have risen superior to the vicissitudes of their ancestors ; men who have contributed to the building up of this great country ; men eminent in science, art and literature; who have become foremost in renown ; even as their ancestors were foremost in battle. The characteristics of their race are not lost, for they still have their true Highland spirit and open-hearted hospitality ; they have neither forgotten the traditions of their ancestors, nor the hereditary Chief or their Clan. My Clansmen, when I return to Scotland I can honestly declare that the sensitive plant, called Clanship, grows and flourishes in this country as our badge, the crowberry, thrives in the Highlands. I can assure them that the love and affection for our race is deeply anchored in your hearts, and that the honor of our Clan is in safe keeping in your hearts. An association has been formed in Glasgow

3

of which I have the honor to be President. Its object is
to preserve records and traditions of the Clan, to render
assistance to members, and to encourage the study of Gaelic
literature. This will keep up the history of our race. Interesting facts are constantly cropping up. I might mention that
Flora MacDonald's faithful maid, Maggie MacEachainn, who
assisted in sheltering Prince Charlie, was a MacLean prior
to her marriage. This I recently discovered from a journal,
written in 1746, which I found in an old house in Forfar-
shire. I should be glad if a similar association was formed
in this country. After the sad events following Culloden, we
all know how scattered the Clan became. No doubt many
of my hearers owe their residence in this country to the
exodus from Scotland in 1746. None suffered more than the
MacLeans. I would not be unmindful of my responsibility
as Chief of this noble Clan. I shall ever endeavor to gain
and retain the confidence of my Clan, and be considered
worthy of wearing three eagles' plumes in my bonnet, which
my ancestors have worn with honor. My Clansmen, there
is a request I have to make before the Atlantic again divides
us, for alas, my residence amongst you must be short. It is
my heart's desire that this noble Clan never forgets the race
you belong to, nor the name you bear. Let the world know
that to bear that name is sufficient passport for nations to
trade with you, to respect you, and to feel that in every
transaction he who bears that name is upright, honest, and
possessed of all the trustworthy qualities which make public
life honorable and our own homes happy. I thank you for
the patience you have displayed in listening to my remarks.
It has been a great pleasure to me to have this privilege of
addressing those of my own name, who belong to my own
race, and who are related to me by more than bonds of
friendship. I have spoken with much diffidence and restraint,

for at this great gathering there are men of letters, historians, professors, and bards, who might justly criticise what I, as a soldier and no orator, might say; but I feel that my Clansmen will make allowance for my failings. Once again I thank you from my heart for the great honor you have conferred on me, and for this unparalleled demonstration, and I assure you that never to the end of my life will the memory of this day be effaced from my mind. May the American and Highland eagles ever soar together in peace and harmony.

This address was received with great enthusiasm, after which loud calls were made for MacLean of Pennycross, who responded as follows:

President, Clanswomen and Clansmen of MacLean:

I am no great speaker, but I am a Highlander of the most genuine stamp—" O mhullach mo chinn gu bhuinn ma bhoun," as we say in Gaelic (from the crown of my head to the sole of my foot)—and you may believe that I feel both proud and pleased at finding myself in such a company as this, when I remember how far a cry it is from Chicago to Texas, San Francisco, and last, but not least, the home of our ancestors, the old Isle of Mull. The MacLeans, the grand old Clan to which we belong, have ever been known not only for prowess in battle, but for high intellectual powers, and for a steadfastness in friendship, and a warm-heartedness of which I have personally felt the pleasing effects since I first set my foot on American soil. It is a well-known fact that all over the world wherever you meet with a MacLean you meet with a gentleman, and with one who, amid all the vicissitudes of life in a foreign land, has never forgotten that guide of descent which goes so far in making a man what he ought

to be—upright, honest, trustworthy and true.   I feel quite
assured that if on this great occasion there should be a scribe
amongst us—even a very ordinary *senachie* could hardly go
wrong—his account of the magnificent reception we are now
receiving at your hands must outstrip anything described by
Boswell.   In Scotland, a short time since, we reckoned on
being able to turn out something like sixteen thousand Mac-
Leans, but across here, all told, you seem to think that more
than twice that number might be mustered without difficulty.
In the time of the Peninsular War my father used to say he
thought our Clan did very well when out of 110 officers
contributed by Mull—a list of whom I now hold in my
hand*—no fewer than 60 were MacLeans, mostly close
relatives, too, of our own family.   This does not include
privates from the Island.   But imagine if you can how old
Gillean of 1174, "Ian Dhu," or "Lachlan Mor" of Duard,
would have felt to think when sorely pressed in this day
by Campbells and Macdonalds, of the possible prospect of
relief by even such a substantial contingent of Clansmen
from beyond the seas as I now see before me.

---

* The following is the list of MacLean officers referred to by Pennycross, who
served in the British army between the years 1800 and 1815, and were from the
Isle of Mull: From Pennycross ·Lieut. Gen. A. T. MacLean (13th Hussars), Capt.
Charles MacLean (79th Highlanders), Lieut. John MacLean (2nd West Indian Regiment), Lieut. Lachlan MacLean (Rifles), Commissary General Assistant Deputy,
Archibald D MacLean ; from Ardfenaig — Capt. Dugald MacLean (Argyleshire
Regiment), Capt. Allan MacLean (90th Regiment), Lieut. John MacLean (6th Regi-
ment), Lieut. Donald MacLean (74th Regiment), Lieut. Niel MacLean (Royal Navy) ;
from Moinechuich   Capt. Allan MacLean ; from Bunessan — Inspector General
Dr. Charles MacLean, Capt. Hector MacLean (93rd Regiment), Lieut. Allan MacLean
(91st Regiment) ; from Uisken — Colonel Alexander MacLean (86th Regiment), Capt.
John MacLean (56th Regiment), Lieut. Archibald MacLean (56th Regiment), Lieut.
Duncan MacLean (56th Regiment) ; from Scoar — Colonel Archibald MacLean) 79th
Regiment), Lieut. Hugh LacLean ; from Torranbeag — Colonel Charles MacLean
(Inspector General of Cavalry), Colonel Alexander MacLean (2nd West Indian Regi-
ment), Lieut. Colonel Archibald MacLean (Cavalry), Captain Allan MacLean (84th
Regiment) ; from Torraneachdrach — Lieut. John MacLean (24th Regiment) ; from
Rossal— Lieut. Duncan MacLean (79th Regiment), Dr. Allan MacLean (The Royals) :
from Ccannagharaair — Capt. Peter MacLean (64th Regiment), Dr. John MacLean

Ladies and gentlemen of MacLean, in the tuneful words of my friend, the bard of Ledaig, Argyllshire,

'S mo chead's an trasd do thir nam buagh so
'S mo bheannachd buan leis an t sluagh tha ann,
'S an cliu a fhuar sinn o linn ar sinnsir
Gu ceann ar criche nach dealaich ruinn,

which have been translated by another friend, not only of myself, but of all Highlands — Professor Blackie —

My blessing be with you brave land and brave people,
In the bright roll of story is blazoned your name,
And may the fair fame of our forefathers never
Be blurred with dishonor or blotted with shame.

I feel myself quite unequal to the task of adequately thanking you for the great honor you have done us, but trust in the interval of time at our disposal before dispersing to have numerous opportunities of acknowledging in a more direct and personal manner your much-valued and never-to-be-forgotten kindness.

Pennycross then concluded with a few warm-hearted Gaelic remarks which were highly appreciated by the old Gaelic-speaking members present, and touched their hearts in a way no English could.

(East Indian Company); from Quinish — General Sir Hector MacLean, Major Norman MacLean, Capt. Hugh MacLean (Foot Guards), Capt. Allan MacLean, Lieut. John MacLean, Capt. Hugh McLean ; from Oscamull — Colonel Hugh MacLean, Captain Hector MacLean, Major Murback MacLean ; from Laggan (Ulva) — Capt. Archibald MacLean (86th Regiment), Capt. Lachlan MacLean (71st Regiment) ; from Torloisk — General Lachlan MacLean (60th Regiment), General MacLean-Cleffin (Guards); from Eansay — Lieut. Hector MacLean, Lieut. Allan MacLean ; from Langamull — Major Donald MacLean (Royals), Lieut. Hugh MacLean (90th Regiment), Dr. Alexander MacLean (East Indian Company); from Brolas — General Sir Fitzroy Grafton Mac-Lean (84th Regiment), Colonel Sir Charles Fitzroy MacLean (84th Regiment) ; from Pennygowan — Lieut. Alexander MacLean (Canadians); from Lochbuie — Captain Murdock MacLean (84th Regiment), Lieut. John MacLean (73rd Regiment), Lieut. Murdock MacLean (42nd Regiment); from Scalesdale — Lieut. General Sir Arch. MacLean (94th Regiment), Colonel Hector MacLean (57th Regiment), Major MacLean (73rd Regiment), and Ensign Lachlan MacLean (3rd West Indian Regiment).

At the conclusion of the speech of Pennycross, the Toast Master, Mr. Charles R. McLain, demanded the attention of the audience by saying: We have present with us a Clansman well-known to you all, and to whom we owe largely this gathering. I now have the pleasure of introducing to you Professor J. P. MacLean, who will respond to the toast, "The Clan MacLean." Professor MacLean made the following address:

THE CLAN MACLEAN.

PROF. J. P. MacLEAN (Greenville, O.).

Mr. President and Members of the Clan :

The honor of responding to the toast, "The Clan MacLean," has been bestowed upon me. I am fully conscious that any eulogium pronounced by me will not add to the glory and honor achieved by our ancestors. It was with many misgivings and much trepidation that I consented to perform this task, for I felt I could not do justice, when I considered that such distinguished men as Professor John Stuart Blackie, Sir Walter Scott, and other noted historians, had bestowed upon our Clan their unstinted praise, and had borne honorable testimony to the devotion, loyalty, intelligence, self-sacrifice and integrity of the heroic sons of the race of Gillean. In view of what has been written by disinterested parties, I know I cannot rise equal to the occasion, for of necessity my words must be wanting in power. And yet, a Clan whose deeds and heroism have been preserved in story and song, needs no words of praise from one who is associated to it by ties of kinship. A Clan that has played an important part in shaping the history of such a romantic country as Scotland is sure to call forth admiration. A Clan that can boast of the valor and fidelity of its warriors on the field of

J. P. MacLean.

Largs, Bannockburn, Harlaw, Inverlochy, Flodden Field, Glenlivat, Inverkeithing, Killiecrankie, Sheriffmuir, and Culloden ; a Clan whose whole line of Chiefs has been intrepid warriors from the beginning to the present, and who have received encomiums from Scotland's greatest historians ; a Clan that can point with pride to its present Chief, knowing him to be a gentleman, a scholar, and a warrior of superior abilities, respected and loved by his Clansmen on account of his energies and devotion to their interests, may well rest content with the place assigned it in Highland history. It is pleasant to contemplate that, although five generations of fighting men have come and gone since the disastrous battle of Culloden, which ended that patriarchal system that bound the Clansmen together in united brotherhood, there remains fraternal greetings and a devoted interest in each other's personal welfare wherever the name of MacLean is known.

The battle of Culloden, already mentioned, not only dates the close of an important epoch in Scotland's history, but marks a period fraught with disastrous results to the Highlands, which eventually ended in cruel evictions and an estrangement of the people. Whatever may have been the consequences of the unfortunate 16th April, 1746, no true Highlander need be ashamed of the conduct of those who took an active part in the battle—enlisted in the cause of Prince Charlie. The revolution of 1745 was the grandest exhibition of chivalry the world has ever witnessed. In the light of more recent events, it may be safely affirmed, that had the Clans been led by a Bonnie Dundee, victory would have perched upon their banner.

The times were not propitious for the MacLeans. Before them was a powerful and hostile Clan, behind them the ceaseless surges of the Atlantic Ocean, and their Chief confined in the Tower of London. Although the great struggle of their prince was a hopeless one, yet this generous Clan rallied to the number of five hundred, and under the leadership of the redoubtable old warrior, Charles Maclean of Drimnin, cut their way through their foes, and with banners flying, eager for the fray, formed in line for the final struggle. They were on the extreme left of the army, and gallantly charged into the ranks of the enemy, leaving not only nearly all their leaders, but also the gentlemen composing the front ranks, to the number of two hundred, dead upon the field.

Nor should it be forgotten that the approach of the enemy was first noticed by Jessie Maclean, who lost no time in warning the patriot army, and thus, in a measure, prepared them for the conflict. Properly speaking, the battle of Culloden ended the days of Clanship. We are to view our Clan as a distinctive tribe, from the days of old Dougall of Scone (1100 A. D.), who has been described as "an influential, just and venerable man," down to Sir Hector the XXI., Chief of MacLean.

Historians and poets have given to the Clan the noblest characteristics, and one of the most frequent designations in Scottish poetry is "The True MacLean." The quality of being true is an exalted possession. In friendship, in loyalty, in hospitality, and in whatever was deemed to be right, the Clan never wavered. The whole line of Chiefs, and the gentlemen of the Clan, were guided by a sublime sense, which fully exemplified itself upon every occasion. Undoubtedly, to this sense the Clan owes its reputation to be a warrior race.

The pride of mankind has led him to deeds of renown. The Highlanders were prone to take up the claymore, and the Clansmen were summoned together by the fiery cross. I think the truth of history will prove that the MacLeans were not a warrior class from choice, but from necessity. On first view this might seem disproved that they were among the

first to take up arms, foremost in battle, and the last to leave
the field of carnage. Ever since the days of Clanship, the
British army has been augmented by this valorous race. But
it must be remembered that in feudal times, when the government was impotent, every Chief was compelled to protect
his vassals from the inroads of his neighbors. The estates
of the MacLeans were bordered by a Clan not disposed to be
peaceable, and hence the art of war became the safeguard to
peace. But when called to action no braver men ever stood
in the front line of battle. At the battle of Glenlivat (Oct.
3rd, 1594), the Chief of MacLean, with his Islesmen, long
withstood the shock of the conflict after all others had fled.
At Inverkeithing (July 20th, 1651) the young Chief of Mac-
Lean, with his eight hundred followers, received the shock
of Cromwell's army, nor would they leave their position. Of
their number only forty escaped alive, while eight gentlemen
of the Clan in succession intervened their bodies between
that of their Chief and the shots of the enemy, each exclaim-
ing, "another for Hector."

It is more profitable to look at the pursuits of peace than
the products of war. The MacLeans lived in the country
of Ossian, and were acquainted with the deeds of Fingal.
The mountains and glens of Scotland have long been pro-
ductive of nature's poets. The mountains of Morvern and
the scenery of Mull must have inspired men of genius from
the earliest times. The MacLeans have also been poets. How
many there have been no man knoweth. The names of many
must have been lost in traditionary times. Prof. Magnus
MacLean, lecturer on physics in the University of Glasgow,
in a recent paper on MacLean Bards, commencing with the
year 1537, gives us a short biography, with specimens of
their poety, of forty-six MacLean poets. This is certainly a
formidable array. Poetry, especially pastoral, enters into

the life of a people, and has no little influence in forming
their character. The poems of Ossian moulded the character
of the Highlanders, and the fortitude, valor and long suffer-
ing of that devoted race, to a great extent, must be ascribed
to the venerable bard. A people given to poetry are emo-
tional, the chords are attuned, and such inspiration as is
received leads to better thoughts and nobler lives. If, with
this, the religious sentiment be imbibed, then they partake of
the spirit of devotion.

Devotion may take a wrong direction, as notably instanced
in the loyalty of the Clan MacLean to the House of Stuart.
The struggle in which the Clan was engaged at Bannockburn
was a righteous one, for it meant national liberty. The
magnetism of Bruce was not only his bravery, but his sense
of freedom for his country. Wallace had paved the way.
The House of Stuart, taken as a whole, was not one to be
admired. But the MacLeans were devoted to it, although
at its hands they received nothing but stripes, and no benefits
accrued to them for all the sufferings they endured. It may
be that to those brought up under a monarchial form of
government the dignity of the nation is represented by the
one that wears the crown, and the king stands as the nation
personified. However that may be, our ancestors regarded
the Stuarts to be the rightful sovereigns, and upon that idea
they staked their fortunes and their lives. This fidelity to
a reigning House gave to the race the name of "The True
MacLean."

The true status of a race must be looked at from within.
While the Highlanders were regarded by the outside world
as a rude, wild and savage race, yet the reverse was true.
On the exterior there was the garb of fierceness, but nobler,
truer and warmer hearts never beat in the breasts of men
than those possessed by the warriors of the land of the mist.

Mull may have been designated as "The Isle of Gloom," yet visitors to it were received with the kindest hospitality by the ancient Lords of Duard. These Chiefs were surrounded by a loyal people, and the interest of one was the common property of all. Should one be sick, there was the famous race of Beatons to apply the healing art—a race nurtured and maintained by the Chiefs of MacLean until they became the most noted in Scotland. Did anyone need the consolations of religion, the Chief was the first to fill the parishes with the best pulpit services that the time afforded. In short, whatever progress was made in the nation was soon applied, so far as circumstances would permit, on the estates of the MacLean.

The poets have also called the MacLeans a "generous Clan." It can be said with pride that the whole history of our Clan was marked by generous deeds and a want of selfishness. A selfish man and a true MacLean were incompatible. Naturally they were given to the love of home, and their interests were to make Mull second to no other isle in Scotland. When called to action, even their homes were sacrificed in the interests of their sovereigns. But let it be said to the honor of the Clan that not one of its members ever fawned upon the monarch, or sought emoluments at his hands. They could fight the battles of their country, but never buy recognition at court. They were never two-faced, and to-day, looking back over the whole line of Chiefs, one may behold men guided by sterling integrity—the greatest gift a father can bestow upon his son.

When all these recorded things come up before me, I am able fully to appreciate the words of John Stuart Blackie, the greatest of living Scottish scholars : "There were mighty men in Mull in those days, and the MacLeans were amongst the mightiest. They were amongst the most loyal of the loyal at Bannockburn, and they could not fail to share the sorrows of the uncrowned monarch at Inverkeithing and Culloden. The MacLeans, if not always wise in action, were generous in purpose and noble in conduct."

If the MacLeans had been less brave, less loyal, and possessed of less integrity of character, and had the perfidy to betray their sovereign, and then to turn and fawn upon him and dance attendance at his court, to-day the Chief of MacLean might have worn the robes of a duke. But would he be honored by his Clanemen? Would he be invited to enjoy the hospitality of his Clansmen four thousand miles away from home? At home, those who personally know him best publish to the world these words, of which anyone should be proud: "Their Chief won golden opinions from the Clan and their friends. Their Chief was proud of his Clan, and they were proud of and devoted to their Chief. He was a gentleman, a scholar, and all that a Highland Chief should be."

Mr. Chairman, we honor ourselves when we pay tribute of respect to our worthy line of ancesters. No more is the tramp of the mailed and tartaned warrior heard in the glens of Mull and Morvern. Where once was the devoted partizan and loyal Clansman, may now be found the shepherd and his flock of sheep. Mighty changes have swept over that country since the time that the MacLean was Lord of Duard. When a poet recently viewed the scene, he was forced to indite:

> From rocky Duard, from Mingary grey,
> The terror of the Clans has passed away.
> They sleep, the plaided warriors of MacLean,
> Where dust of battle may not rise again.
> Sheathed is the claymore, vanished from the sea
> The white-winged pride of Ocean chivalry;
> Hushed is the slogan, bloodless flow the waves,
> And death seems buried in those island graves!

The irreparable wrong committed upon the Highlanders has not been without its compensations. Nature is a great mother, and she constantly opens new avenues for her sons and daughters. Fresh Keltic blood must be poured into the sluggish veins of the Saxon and his kindred types. The Scoto-Irish must seek other homes, and in America they have found a genial soil for their energy and enterprise. So the MacLeans, by force of circumstances, driven from their home, have found a habitation wherever civilization extends. In the struggle for existence, he will be found among the foremost in every department of life. But wherever he may be found, he has a warm heart for his Clan, and is proud of the fact that Highland blood courses through his veins. A loyal sentiment has brought us together to-night. We are proud that the MacLean is with us, and that other MacLean of Pennycross, who is equal in birth, equal in virtues to anyone in the Highlands of Scotland. We have partially looked over the past. We honor it. We would make the words of the poet true :

> Their memory warms at old tradition
>   Of Mull, and Coll, and dark Lismore.
> Old Fingal deeds, Culumba's mission,
>   The Duard towns, and Aros shore.
>
> How proud are they of clannish tartan,
>   How dear to them the bonnet blue,
> The Gaels' descendants set their heart on
>   The colors of their fathers true.
>
> In later, as in older, story
>   Of battlefield, the Clan MacLean
> Has borne a greater share of glory
>   Than tamer races of the plain.
>
> Schooled as of old the warrior Spartan,
>   To live and die for home and fame,
> With steel, in blood, these men in tartan
>   On honor's shield have graved their name.

In war, MacLean is brave in battle!
    In peace, a credit to his Clan!
In office, trade, or feeding cattle,
    In love, or friendship, he's your man.

Then blow the pibroch o'er the waters,
    We'll dance a reel with might and main,
Long live the name, the sons, and daughters,
    At home, abroad, of Clan MacLean!

The Toast Master next announced a Gaelic song
entitled, "Ho, Ro', Mo Nighean doun Broidheach," to
be sung by J. W. McLean. In the rendering of this
song Mr. McLean was accompanied by a harp.

THE MACLEANS OF THE UNITED STATES.
Hon. Alex. McLean (Macomb, Ill.).

The third toast of the evening, proposed by the Toast
Master, was "The MacLeans of the United States," and
in introducing the speaker, observed: We have with
us a gentlemen greatly interested in our educational
movement, and, who for several years, has been the
President of the Board of Trustees of the University
of Illinois. I now call upon Hon. Alex. McLean, of
Macomb, Ill., to respond to "The MacLeans of the
United States."

Mr. McLean, addressing the chair, said:

Mr. President:

Forty years ago I left the land of cakes for this land
of corn. This great commonwealth of Illinois then had a
population less than one-half that of the present number in
this goodly city of Chicago. I was a stranger in a strange
land, and so far as I knew, not a MacLean outside my father's

ALEXANDER MCLEAN.

family in the State. It was then I felt like the prophet of old, while in the cave of Mount Horeb, when he exclaimed, "I, even I only am left," believing he was the last of the true worshippers of God. He was commanded to arise and to be of good cheer, for there were 7,000 still living who had not bowed the knee to Baal. Since then I have learned, and now I see I was mistaken, for the MacLeans in the United States are sufficiently numerous to re-people Mull, Coll and Tiree, and some of the adjacent isles of the sea. When I was a lad, in this section of country, there were but two classes of foreigners known, the Dutch and Irish, by the native population, and when I was addressed under either of these names, let me say, the hot MacLean blood rebelled against the impeachment, and the interrogator was reminded of his error in a manner more decisive than polite. In fact, many had never seen a Scotchman, and in some way were impressed with the idea that he had either horns or hoofs, or at least, we were carefully scrutinized from head to foot before we could pass muster. Happily that era has passed, and a Scotchman is now known as a thrifty, cautious, loyal citizen, and obtains at the hands of the people of this nation all the consideration he merits or deserves.

Of late years I have been digging into the history of our Clan, so far as my limited opportunities would permit, and I find that our family name goes very far back in the annals of time, as being a stirring and warlike people, ready at all times to maintain their honor, resent an insult, or assist in a friendly raid, as was the humor of the times; that they were independent, self-reliant, with an excellent opinion of themselves, and proud of their ancestry and their deeds. In fact in my study and investigation I have become impressed with some feelings of pride of ancestry, and in the ancient origin of the Clan, so much so that it would probably not be difficult to convince me that our great ancestor was named *Adam* MacLean. At any rate there is scripture for it that there were *two camels* in the ark, when the great deluge came upon the earth, yet I am aware of the tradition in our family that every MacLean had a boat of their own. Hence, as a matter of course, there was no need to take passage with Captain Noah. Whether the tradition be founded on fact or not, it is true nevertheless, and this goes far to prove that our claim to antiquity must be correct.

History also informs us that the Clan MacLean constituted a large and formidable people in the long ago, and that the normal condition of Clanship enjoyment was *fechting*, and that they had a goodly share of that pastime, and though not always successful, I find they were always loyal to their Chief, and true to the cause in which they were engaged. No traitor or coward was ever found in their ranks. For this we are proud, and to-night, no MacLean at this festal board need blush or be ashamed that they were, as I have said, proud, independent to rashness, with a feeling of personal dignity for their good name, fearing to bring reproach upon their ancestry, and emulous to add lustre to its history and preserve our motto, "Virtue Mine Honor," untarnished. Therefore let us emulate their good deeds, and not quarter our coat of arms with the "bar sinister," but "let the two seals rampant" stand upright, as of yore. Let us be proud and jealous of our name, and bring no dishonor on the fair pages of our history. We should have pride of family, faith in its honor, esteem for its history, and glory in the fact that we belong to the Clan MacLean, and allied to its hereditary Chief.

I am the more impressed to-night with the source of that bond of affection which exists between the Chief and his Clansmen, in contradistinction from the time when the only bond between man and Chief was not blood inherited, but blood shed in a common cause. We are all profoundly impressed with the honor we enjoy to-night in seeing our Chief, Sir Fitzroy Donald MacLean, and Chieftain MacLean of Pennycross and his estimable lady, with us in the flesh. Much have I read, and more have I heard from my father and family, about the head of our Clan, and proud I feel of the name. But it was then a romance, much of fiction and more of a dream. Now all seems to be reality, and well can I understand why it was the MacLeans would so enthusiastically follow their Chief to the field of battle, to the death for weel or woe. When I received the circular announcing that the fiery cross, for the first time since 1745, had been sent out over the hills and valleys of Canada, and the broad prairies of the great Northwest of America, summoning the MacLeans to respond to the call of their Chief to meet him in the City of Chicago, my sluggish blood was aroused, every fiber of my being was awakened, and I made the vow, so well remembered by our noble Chief, that I will obey the summons and meet my Clansmen at the appointed time. I ceased to be plain "Sandy McLean," and became Alexander McLean, the Clansman. While the blood continues to course through my veins, it shall be the honor of my life that I am your Clansman, and this heritage I promise to try and hand down to my children, so that the good name of the family shall not suffer at their hands.

While we are congratulating ourselves on the grand history of our Clan, we must remember that our name is not unknown in the United States. Nay, more, there is not a state or territory in this broad land but has a representative of this prolific family, and, so far as known, will compare favorably with any Clan-name in the roll of American citizenship. In order to condense this part of my remarks, I deem it but

4

simple justice to the learned author and well-known ethnol-
ogist, Prof. J. P. MacLean, the author of that invaluable
work, the "History of the Clan MacLean," to make an
extract from his history, touching the matter of the MacLeans
in the United States, which, after years of careful study and
examination into original documents in Scotland and else-
where, will ever be regarded as authentic. He says : "Sixteen thousand MacLeans still live in Scotland, but very
few on the ancient estates, although they may be found in
Ireland, England, India, the Gold Coast of Africa, the West
Indies, Canada and the United States. Canada and the
United States contain not far from twenty thousand of
the name. In the directory of the city of Philadelphia are
recorded the names of two hundred, probably representing
not less than five hundred. New York adds one hundred
and thirty, representing about four hundred. To give an
account of the MacLeans in America would require a large
volume. They have flourished in the arts, sciences, and the
elements of civilization in this country, surpassing those left
on the native soil. All of the various walks of life have
been adorned by those of the name. They have obtained
eminence in statesmanship, diplomacy, civil law, divinity,
medicine, invention, literature and the fine arts. We have
found MacLeans battling for freedom and winning renown,
not only for daring, but for a patriotism born inherent in
human rights. To speak of those whose voices have been
heard in the halls of Congress, or the acts of those who
have held cabinet positions, or sat in Governors' chairs, or
rendered decisions from the Supreme Court, or engaged in
the diplomatic service, or arousing and instructing the people
from the editor's chair, or spoken words of wisdom and
consolation from the pulpit, or gave sound medical advice,
would be great pleasure, but must require a large volume.

The name has been fully identified in the geography of the United States. Illinois has a McLean County containing 1,155 square miles, with a population of 75,000. In that County is a post-village of the same name. McLeansborough is the County seat of Hamilton County, same State. One of the counties of Western Kentucky is named McLean, and contains 325 square miles, with a population of 7,500. There is a McLean County in Dakota. Minnesota has a McLean Township in Ramsey County. Ohio has a McLean post-office in Fayette County, and a McLean Township in Shelby County. Tompkins County, in New York, has a McLean post-village. McLain is the name of a post-office in Harvey County, Kansas. McLane is a post-office in Erie County, Pennsylvania, and in Crawford County, same State, is McLean's Corners. There is a McLeansville in Guilford County, North Carolina. McLeansville is a village in Jackson County, Tennessee, and McClain's a post-office in Wirt County, West Virginia."

We could not add to this record without being considered vainglorious; but it may be well to say to the Chief that his Clansmen in this country will compare favorably with those in other lands. These Clansmen around you, and "Clanswomen," to borrow an appropriate word from our worthy President, W. A. McLean—and I like it—are men and women of representative character in their various walks of life. If you desire to be at the head of the larger portion of the Clan MacLean, I see no other way than that you locate on this continent. Be that as it may, we here and now renew our fealty to you as the head of our tribe, whether 5,000 miles across the prairies and the sea, or on the shores of the great lake of Illinois, and while we may be sometimes impassioned, hasty or rash, we still will remember the prayer of the old elder, who besought the Lord to keep him *richt*, for when he was *wrang* he was *awfu* wrang.

Finally, my honored Chief, we return you our personal sincere and hearty thanks for your presence here to-night Your Clansmen, who have never seen a Chief before, but have read and cherished the memory of your ancestry with emotions of delight, feel honored by your presence. To you Chieftain MacLean of Pennycross and your estimable lady we also thank you in the sincerity of our hearts for your presence at this Clan gathering. Our heart's desire and prayer to God is, that you will long be spared to be our Chief and Chieftain, and your return to your native land in safety be vouchsafed, and a reunity of the family ties of those you love. Under the providence of God, may this, our meeting, be for the good of us all, believing that we have learned somewhat of our kith and kin, which will tell of our families for years to come.

THE MACLEANS OF CANADA.

Major Hugh H. McLean (St. John, N. B.).

The Toast-Master announced that this toast was to have been responded to by Hon. W. F. Maclean, of Toronto, but owing to his absence, Major Hugh H. McLean had kindly consented to favor us on the above subject. While we are disappointed by the absence of Mr. Maclean of Toronto, yet, I can assure you that his place will be ably filled by Major McLean, whom I now have the pleasure of introducing to you.

In response, Major McLean spoke as follows:

Mr. President, Ladies and Gentlemen:

I regret that the gentleman (Hon. W. F. Maclean, M. P.) who was to respond to this toast is not able to be present, in his hands it would have received due justice.

HUGH H. McLEAN.

I thank you brother Clansmen on behalf of the MacLeans of Canada for the hearty manner in which you received this toast, and for the honor you have done us in proposing it. We are your kinsmen, united to you by the ties of blood and Clan association, descended from the same stock, and coming from the same country. The grand reception we have received here has made us feel that the old feeling of Clan unity has been revived and is again in practical force, and I believe will forever continue. The MacLeans of Canada join with the MacLeans of the United States in welcoming our Chief to this gathering. As in old times our fathers gathered at the Clan call to support and defend with their arms and lives the forefathers of our Chief, so we now come together to renew our allegiance, and to assure him that the old Clan ties bind us as strong to him as they bound our fathers to his.

The earnest and eloquent speech of our Chief has stirred us to unwonted enthusiasm ; let us not forget his advice, but with all our strength endeavour to be " True MacLeans." Let us teach our children the noble traditions of our Clan, and instill into their hearts maxims of honor and right, so that they may keep the name unsullied, and prove to the world that they are worthy of the name MacLean.

We must be true to our country, true to our friends, and true to ourselves in order to be " True MacLeans."

It has always been the proud boast of our Clan that the MacLeans are not traitors. Carry out this principle in the ordinary every-day affairs of life and prove to our fellow citizens that the descendants of the men who fought at Culloden are true, faithful and firm friends.

The MacLeans of Canada are noted for their loyalty and love of their country. We are British subjects, and are happy to live under the glorious flag of the Empire. We are proud to be called Canadians, to be the defenders and guardians of half a continent—a land of unbounded promise and predestined renown—a country to live for and to die for. My friend on my right says: "Your country is not an independent State." I say we are a State. "What constitutes a State? Not turret or embattled tower, but men. Free-born men who know their rights, and will defend them. These constitute a State."

We are no longer a congeries of disconnected provinces, destitute of any strong hand of sympathy, or mutual attachments. We are a united country, developing into a great State without the instrumentality of the sword. The name of MacLean is interwoven in the history of Canada. General Francis MacLean was, in 1778, Commander-in-chief of the forces in Nova Scotia, and in 1779 defended successfully the Penobscot against the Americans.

General Allan MacLean defended Quebec, in 1776, from an attack on it made by the Americans under Montgomery and Benedict Arnold, and by his pluck and skill saved Quebec. A score of other names could be mentioned, but the hour is late and I will not weary you with an account of their services. I must, however, not forget to mention that our honored President was born in Canada, and that our esteemed Vice-President, Dr. Donald MacLean, of Detroit, is also a Canadian. I was told to-day that Dr. MacLean stands next to the Chiefship after the house of our present Chief.

And now let me conclude by thanking the MacLeans of Chicago for their kindness to us Canadians during our visit to this great city. They have well carried out the traditions of the Clan in the lavish hospitality they have shown us.

To the gentlemen who organized this association and gave us the pleasure of meeting our Chief and forming new friendships, our heartiest thanks are extended. To Prof. MacLean, our historian, we say you are a "True MacLean." I understand my friend Hector MacLean, of Nova Scotia, has been selected to move a special vote of thanks to the Professor, so I will leave to him to express our feelings of respect and gratitute.

Our meeting has been a grand success, but there is one member of our Clan absent who should be present to make it a complete success. I refer to the Rev. MacLean Sinclair, of Prince Edward Island, the Canadian depository of the MacLean history, who is in fact, a walking encyclopædia of all facts relating to our Clan.

Clansmen, in a few hours this re-union will be at an end; in a few days we shall have returned to our homes, and be again scattered over the length and breadth of this great continent. Shall we dissolve this Association now, and consider this a final meeting of the MacLeans of America, or shall we make this a permanent organization. (Loud cries of assent were heard from those present.) I am glad you affirm so decidedly and strongly the principle that this Association must be permanent. This will bring us in accord with our brothers in Scotland, who have a similar Association there. I will therefore move the following resolutions :

Resolved—That the MacLeans of North America form themselves into an Association to be called "The Clan Mac-'Lean."

And Further Resolved—That the officers of the Association of the Clan MacLean of Chicago be the officers of the said Clan until its next meeting.

And Further Resolved—That the said officers be, and they are hereby, empowered to make the necessary Constitution and By-Laws for said Clan.

And be it Further Resolved—That the next Annual Meeting of the Clan be held in the City of Toronto, next year, at a date to be fixed by said officers.

These resolutions were seconded by quite a number, and, on being put by the presiding officer, were carried unanimously.

Hector MacLean, of Bridgetown, N. S., then offered the following motion :

" I move that the thanks of the MacLeans be tendered to Prof. J. P. MacLean for the valuable services he has rendered the Clan."

The Chief arose and requested permission to second the motion.   The motion having been put, was carried unanimously.   .

THE MACLEANS OF CHICAGO.
Hon. Donald McLean (New York.).

Charles R. McLain in proposing this toast, remarked that the gentleman who accompanied the Chief from New York to Chicago will respond to the next sentiment, and has come a long distance to speak to you. Although the hour is somewhat late, you will be well repaid by attentively listening to Hon. Donald McLean, whom I now present to you.

Mr. McLean responded :

Mr. President, Ladies and Gentlemen :

I must, first of all, correct the erroneous impression the introduction of our urbane Toast Master would leave you under.   Of all the motives that led me to take the journey

DONALD McLEAN.

from New York to meet my kinsmen from all parts of America in this great gathering of our Clan, I can assure you that the purpose of making a speech was not one of them.

When, two days ago, the efficient committee having charge of the arrangements here asked if I, when called upon, would say a word about the "MacLeans of Chicago," the coy manner in which the request was made clearly indicated to me that a New Yorker was selected because the MacLeans of Chicago shared, with all other residents of this city, that modesty which is so characteristic of all Chicagoians, and could not, therefore, themselves remind us of the debt we owe them for the pleasures of this week, I gladly accepted. For the benefit of those of you who are not aware of the fact, I would explain here that there is supposed to exist a feeling of rivalry between that city, which we New Yorkers still consider the Metropolis of the nation, and this great city of the "Wild West," and that upon every fitting occasion the residents of each are supposed to ridicule the pretensions of the other. Therefore, when I entered this banquet hall, and found my name printed as one to respond to a formal toast, I knew that this was my opportunity. But, owing to the lateness of the hour, and other considerations more potent still, I have concluded to forego the privilege which the occasion seems to afford. But before resuming my seat, I wish to relate an incident in my journey hither, and this for the pleasure of my Chicago friends.

It fell to my lot, as you know, to accompany our beloved Chief from New York to this city, an honor I highly appreciated, affording a pleasure I shall never forget; but, on the trip, Sir Fitzroy, unwittingly, I am sure, but none the less keenly, wounded me. After we had travelled an hour or two, I discovered from the tenor of his remarks, that the Chief supposed we were about approaching Chicago. Knowing, as I did, that there prevails in the minds of most

cultivated Englishmen a very vague idea of the geography
of our great land, and that the names of such of our cities
as are known to them at all are supposed to designate the
various suburbs of New York. I thought to correct the
erroneous impression conceived by me to exist in the Chief's
mind, by explaining that New York was a thousand miles
from Chicago. Imagine my feelings when, by his reply,
he disclosed the fact that his impressions, though fully as
erroneous, were quite the opposite of what I had supposed.
His reply, uttered with a tone of genuine surprise was,
" Why in the world does Chicago *have* her landing station
so far away ? "

But, seriously, my friends, late as is the hour, I must ask
you to consider the debt of gratitude we owe for the privilege
of participating in this unique gathering, and to whom we
owe it.

Sir Fitzroy has most fittingly, and with feelings evidently
from the heart, expressed the pride he owns at being the
chief guest of honor here. Surely he does well to feel
so. He were something less than the gentleman of refined
sensibilities we have found him to be, did not his heart swell
with pride at the sight of this gathering of his Clansmen of
America. The more remarkable does it seem when it is
remembered that very many of us are removed by several
generations from natives of the Old Land, and that many
more of us have never had the romantic inspiration that
comes with a vision of its rugged hills, its shaded glens and
mirrored lakes, that we should come together, from every
section of this great land, with hearts as loyal to our Chieftain as were those of our forefathers when summoned by the
fiery cross.

The MacLeans of Chicago have given us the occasion to
see their great " White City," a veritable pageantry of the

whole world, the like of which has never before been seen. They have given us the opportunity to know and welcome with loyal affection Sir Fitzroy Donald MacLean, Chief of the Clan, in whose personality we have realized our most romantic ideal of what should make a great Chief of the greatest Clan: the brave soldier, the cultured gentleman ; and second only to the Chief of the Clan, the pleasure of knowing, which means the opportunity to love, the stalwart Chieftain of Pennycross and his good lady, who so charmingly supplements the good fellowship of his own genial personality.

For the pleasure of these privileges, the MacLeans of New York have the liveliest sense of the debt they owe, and I am sure that I but express the feelings of every man and woman here when I return our heartfelt thanks to those who made possible, and carried to so brilliant a success, this gathering—the subject of our toast, "The MacLeans of Chicago."

THE LAND OF OUR ANCESTORS AND THE LAND WE LIVE IN.
REV. CALVIN B. McLEAN (Simsbury, Conn.).

You are next invited, said the Toast-Master, to listen to a gentleman who lives in Connecticut, who has something, I am sure, worth listening to, and upon a subject of interest to all. I take the pleasure in calling upon Rev. Calvin B. McLean, who will respond to the toast, " The Land of our Ancestors and the Land we Live In." Standing beside the Toast-Master, Mr. McLean said:

Mr. President, Clansmen and Clanswomen :

In response to this toast, "The Land of our Ancestors and the Land we Live In," you call forth the throbbing senti‐ ments that come down to us to-night in Chicago, this city of cities, in these United States, this country of countries, from all the ages past.

It was hardly becoming to me to accept this duty, but coming from a long ancestral line of those who never flinched in any duty, but dare even to die for the honor of the name we all love, I knew not how to turn my back on this service.

It is the highest privilege of my life, dear Clansmen, to sit with you here in the presence of our noble hereditary Chief, whom we delight to honor, and the heads of families — branches of our most beloved Clan MacLean ; and by reviving a love for our fathers and the lands of our fathers, and quicken the love for our brothers and Clansmen the world over, we cannot but feel our hearts burn within us as with an interest never before felt, we sing over the old songs, tell over the old tales, and write at the end of each our Clan motto, " Virtue Mine Honor."

If, as in boyhood, I climbed to the top of a mountain and looked away to the eastward, wondering what lay beyond, to-night turn to the lands of our ancestors, I see nearest the little State of Connecticut, then the island of Coll, then

> "The Isles that stud the stormy waters
> Of Caledonia's rugged strands."

But back, back through the centuries our line of descent goes unbroken, and before the Christian era our ancestral halls in Scotia were trod by bravest sons and daughters of the Clan MacLean. But long before that time, as the great waves of population pressed out from the vast Asiatic hive, they traversed Europe, leaving on every hand traces of their skill, we must know that all Europe has felt the touch of power of those whose family motto is, and ever shall be, " Virtue Mine Honor."

If we turn to sacred story, and, like the ancient Hebrew,

trace along the line backward, we come to Noah and the
flood, and then there comes to our lips unbidden the dear
old legend, that "The MacLean was there, and he had a boat
of his ain," with the thistle upraised for an ensign, and
in characters we now decipher was the same grand motto,
"Virtue Mine Honor." But whence came he? We pore
over the Holy Book, and read of Enoch who "Walked with
God, and was not, for God took him." And as we know in
our own experiences, as well as from the sacred book, that
the "God of our fathers" changes not in all the ages, but
has a ceaseless care for his own, we can easily believe that
this ancient legend has more than doubtful proof that the
sons of Enoch who followed in the footsteps of their father,
and feared the Lord, were not all drowned in the flood, and
that it might have been, nay, is even probable, that the Mac-
Lean did have "a boat of his own," as well as father Noah.

If we go back from this, it is easy to trace to one who
was contemporaneous with Adam as our ancestors made in
God's image, in the sweet valley of Eden so long ago.

But, Mr. President, of which of these lands of our ancestors
would you have me speak. Eden, the mother of the nations,
Europe, the halting place of restless, energetic and ambitious
Clansmen, or Bonnie Scotland, and

"The Isles of the West, lovely Isles of the West,
As emeralds set in the blue ocean's breast,
The birth place of Clansmen war-nurtured and brave,
The home where the tempest-king rides on the waves ;
Where thunders roll on in their terrible might,
And keen lightnings dance on each peak with delight ;
Where morning's dawn-rays o'er the mountain crests run,
And gloaming descends as a sigh from the sun ;
When pale ghosts career in the mist-shrouded hills,
And heard are the wails in the songs of the rills ;
Where beauty is shrined in each lone grassy vale,

And wee flowerets laugh to the voice of the gale ;
Where unfettered peace as a heaven presides,
And Nature's sweet loveliness ever abides ;
Where maidens and youths, round their dim cottage fires,
Exultingly tell of the deeds of their sires ;
Or sing with emotion the grand battle lays,
Of heroes who fought in the far-away days,
For King and for Chieftain, for honor and love,
For aught that would valor or dignity prove.
O, Isles of the West, ever bosomed in song,
My Highland harp whispers — the sound I'll prolong ;
Speak on, my dear harp ; list, it trembles again,
'Tis 'Virtue Mine Honor' and dauntless MacLean."

Such descriptions of the lands of our ancestors, by one
who *saw* whereof she wrote, fill us with gladness to-day, and
though many have not seen, yet from childhood's days, we
have intuitively loved the names of all the Western Isles
and coasts — ever the home of the MacLeans.

But when we think of the Scot's Land, there come up to
us not only the breezy lochs and echoing vales, the rock-
ribbed hills, but the heather and moors, of which poets have
sung, and song-writers have set in quaintest tunes the simple
tales, like "Come O'er the Sea, Charlie," and "Robin Adair,"
with such singular uniqueness that all the world praise while
they enjoy the old songs.

If we speak of the Kirk, the schools, the castle, or the
cottages that commonly in all the centuries have *there* been
friends, we can understand how our ancestors, coming down
from all the Hebrew race and language, have been renowned
as watchful students of "God's letter to His children," and
have been noted as deep scholars and earnest followers of
the Divine teachings. So we can understand, when they
have been scattered in all lands, why they have, as single
individuals, been as so many grains of salt, conserving ever

and always the best and holiest interests of the communities in which they dwelt.

But while our thought goes over and over again "The Tales of a Grandfather," and the feuds and wars that so decimated the ranks of the brave and noble Clan MacLean : while we cannot but refer to the barbarian cruelties practiced by evictions, to drive out the crofters and compel removals to strange and far-off lands, even in late years. We can, most of us, turn with the old-time loyalty to the true, to the lands we live in with a smile on our faces, and a purpose to do our part as true MacLeans in every emergency of political strife or civil environment, or theological differences, and *stand by that which is good*, and that which will produce the greatest good to the greatest number, whether in Scotland, or in Europe, Australia or India, the Dominion of Canada or the States. I make no discrimination between those of us whose homes are in the Dominion or the States. We, as a race, are equally loyal to the great principles of a free government for the people, and by the people.

But, sir, I must not trespass on the time. Having met together to-night we shall never be the same men and women we have been ; our views of life and of Clanship have widened. To-night we fashion a golden chain of friendship, which, strengthened by the silvery cord of memory, will stretch from ocean to ocean, from time to eternity ; but it can never break.

Chieftain, Clansmen :

May dear and lovely Scotland, and the lovely Isles as well,
Our own beloved Homeland, and every State where dwell
The true and loyal Clansmen, hear the heart-throbs of our joy,
As we weld the links of friendship, with blood the sole alloy ;
Let sweet and tender memories, like silver cords entwine,
The deathless fame, and peerless names, along the ancestral line ;
Our children learn that deeds and worth, have never been in vain,
So let each son most worthy be, who bears the name MacLean.

THE HEROIC WOMEN OF THE MACLEANS.

DR. DONALD MACLEAN (Detroit, Mich.).

We have now come to the last address of the evening, said the Toast-Master. We are about to listen to a gentleman who has made a name for himself in medicine and surgery. I ask your attention while Dr. Donald MacLean addresses us on "The Heroic Women of the MacLean."

Mr. President, Clansmen and Clanswomen :

Leaving out of consideration for the present those grand characters who in the past have helped to write the name of our Clan on the scroll of fame, and added in that way a glorious page to the history of Scotland, premit me on the present occasion to direct the attention of my Clansmen and Clanswomen to a special class of heroic women whose lives and labors, if less conspicious and less known to the world at large, were no less honorable to themselves, and no less glorious in their true heroism and their services to humanity than the other and more prominent class. I refer to that class so touchingly and truly described in the beautiful Scotish lyric, with which, I have no doubt, you are all familiar :

> The morn was fair, the skies were clear,
>   No breath came o'er the sea,
> When Mary left her Highland cot
>   And wandered forth with me.
>
> The flowers decked the mountain side,
>   And fragrance filled the vale ;
> By far the fairest flower there
>   Was the Rose of Allandale.
>
> When'er I wandered, east or west,
>   When fate began to lower,
> A solace still was she to me
>   In sorrow's lonely hour.

DONALD MacLEAN, M. D.

When tempests lashed our gallant bark,
  And rent her shivering sail,
One maiden form withstood the storm —
  'Twas the Rose of Allandale.

And when my fevered lips were parched
  On Afric's burning sand,
She whispered hopes of happiness
  And tales of distant land.

My life had been a wilderness,
  By fortune's gales unblest,
Had fate not linked my fate with her's —
  The Rose of Allandale.

It is for those women of our Clan who have gone forth from their Highland homes, sometimes with members of their own Clan, sometimes as helpmate and companion to members of other Clans and other families, and in the wilds of America, in the deserts of India, in short, in every land and every clime, have lived the lives and wielded the influence for good that vindicates their title to the rank and fame of the true heroine. It is, I say, for this class that in all confidence I ask your loving and grateful consideration on this joyous occasion.

I would like, if time permitted, to sketch briefly for you the chief points in the eventful career of one such individual of this class of heroines. The one, viz., of whom I know most, and of whom I have the best right to speak, the one who has watched over and cared for and guided and helped my life from the moment I drew my first breath even until now, and to whom I am indebted for anything in the way of success or usefulness which I may have achieved. Born and brought up in the midst of all the romantic and inspiring surroundings of her Highland home in the Isle of Mull, from the loving recollections of which I know that she was able

5

to evolve thoughts and suggestions which cheered and supported heart and soul, and carried her safely through a long life of more than ordinary vicissitudes and trial, and, I may add, usefulness.

Married about the age of seventeen, under the guiding influence (as she has always believed) of two supreme directing powers, viz., first, the hand of " Him who doeth all things well," and second, the irresistible power of romantic Higland love. With the husband of her choice, who had had the great misfortune to lose his eyesight in boyhood, with him she emigrated to the backwoods of America, with the firm determination to overcome all obstacles, and by brave united effort, to hew out and build up a local habitation and a name for themselves.

Nor was this determination ever shaken or departed from ; on the contrary, all that it involved, including losses by fire, by tempest, by shipwreck, by sickness, by affliction, was met with the fidelity, the patience, the unflinching courage of the true heroine, until now, at the age of 74, from the quiet, peaceful home in the bosom of her family, surrounded by many children and grand-children, she authorizes me to convey to you, her Clansmen and Clanswomen assembled here, her cordial greeting, and I am sure I may truthfully add the benediction, not only of a true heroine, but of a good old woman.

It would be very difficult to over-estimate the value to the many people in many lands whose lives have been touched and elevated by the benign influences of such examples as the heroic women of our Clan have each one, in her own special sphere, furnished wherever her lot has been cast. My only regret is that this important and inspiring toast had not been allotted to some one more competent to do it the justice it deserves.

After drinking to the health of the Chief, Penny-cross and lady, and Lady MacLean, the banqueters adjourned to their several places of entertainment.

VII. — THE CONCERT.

An invitation having been received from the Armour Packing Company to visit their industry, a special train was furnished by the Lake Shore and Michigan Southern Railway, and at nine o'clock a. m., of the 16th, the MacLeans left the Rock Island Depot for the stockyards, slaughter and packing houses of the Armour Company. A guide was furnished the party, and two assistant superintendents went along to give information. At one o'clock p. m., the party returned to Headquarters. The rooms were kept open until five o'clock p. m.

The festivities were to conclude by a concert, given in Central Music Hall, at eight o'clock p. m. This was to be held jointly by the MacLean Association and the Highland Association of Illinois. The programme was as follows:

1. Organ Voluntary (with Scotch Melodies), ... Miss Viola McLean
2. Selected Airs, ... 48th Highlanders' Pipe Band, Toronto
3. Vocal Solo — "Come O'er the Stream, Charlie, ...
.... Miss Helen Maclean
4. Vocal Solo — "The Highlandman's Toast," .... Wm. MacKenzie
5. Recitation — "The Dowie Dens of Yarrow," .... T. W. Stewart
6. Violin Solo — "Scotch Fantasia," .... Charles D'Almaine
7. Vocal Solo — "Land of the Leal," .... MacKenzie Gordon
8. Dance — "Highland Fling," .... Fred Riddle
9. Vocal Solo — "My Heart's in the Highlands," Miss Viola McLean
10. Selections, ... 48th Highlanders' Pipe Band

11. Vocal Solo — " Robin Adair,"............Miss Carrie Baenziger
12. Vocal Solo — "Scots Wha Hae,".............Wm. MacKenzie
13. Recitation — "Geordie Johnstone,".............T. M. Stewart
14. Humorous Song — "Oh, Johnny, You're a Dandy,"......
....A. S. Macreadie
15. Solo — "Mary of Argyle,"................MacKenzie Gordon
16. Violin Selections,........................Charles D'Almaine
17. Dance — "Sword Dance,".....................Fred Riddle
18. Song and Chorus — "Will ye no Come Back Again,"....
....Miss Viola McLean

As every one of the participants was encored, it
would prove that their performance was not only well
executed, but there was also an appreciative audience.
The MacLeans turned out to the concert in full force.
Many were noticed in the audience who had not attended
the previous meetings.

VIII. — REMARKS.

Many of the MacLeans now took their departure for
their respective homes. Others remained longer, that
they might continue to visit the World's Columbian
Exposition for a few days.

The Chief of the Clan took his departure for home,
going by the way of Toronto. Here a banquet was
given him on Monday evening, June 26th, which was
fully reported in *The Scottish Canadian* of the 29th.
From there he proceeded to New York, and was again
entertained by the Clansmen. On July 5th he sailed
on board the Steamship Germanic for Liverpool. In
a private letter to Mrs. J. P. MacLean—the latest
advice received from him—we are informed that he
reached Queenstown on July 12th. In the letter he

takes occasion to say: "I deeply appreciate the courtesy my Clansmen showed me and the warm-hearted reception I received. I must express my regret that I was unable to converse with many of the older members of the Clan, who, in spite of their age, came from far and wide to welcome their Chief."

The Chieftain MacLean of Pennycross remained in Chicago for several days, that he might the more leisurely take in the Columbian Exposition and view such places of interest as Chicago afforded. From there he went to Detroit. On July 12th he arrived, accompanied by Mrs. MacLean, at Greenville, Ohio, where he took a much needed rest. July 19th, he left for Toronto, where, at this writing, he now is.

The weather during the festival was all that could be desired. The exposition was nearly completed.

The Chief and Chieftain made a very favorable and lasting impression on their Clansmen. All were free to express their feelings, and declared an honorable pride in the distinguished guests.

It was a matter of some pride to the writer of this, in looking into the faces of those at the banquet, to recognize that nearly all either possessed a copy, or else had read, his "History of the Clan MacLean,"

A LIST OF THOSE PRESENT AT THE BANQUET.

I have put forth every endeavor to make this list complete. Seventy of the names I was able to call; several I have added after an extensive correspondence, and a few were afforded from the treasurer's books. About one-third I have been unable to secure. Believing the list should be preserved, I give it in this incomplete state:

Sir Fitzroy Donald MacLean, Bart., Chief of the Clan,......
Archibald John MacLean of Pennycross,..................
Mrs. MacLean of Pennycross,...........................
J. O. Maclean,................Los Angeles, Cal.
Dr. Robert A. McLean,........San Francisco, Cal.
Mrs. Robert A. McLean,.......   "   "   "
M. H. DeYoung,...............   "   "   "
Mrs. M. H. DeYoung,.........   "   "   "
Major Hugh H. McLean,.......St. John, N. B., Canada.
Mrs. Hugh H. McLean,........   "   "   "   "
Harry P. McLean,............   "   "   "   "
Hector MacLean,.............Bridgetown, N. S.,   "
Miss Jarvis Flora Maclean,.....Guelph, Ont., Canada.
Allan MacLean,.............Kingston, Ont., Canada.
W. A. McLean,.............Owen Sound, Ont., Canada.
Frank W. McLean,...........Toronto, Ont., Canada.
Lieut. Hugh C. McLean,.......   "   "   "
Capt. J. B. McLean,..........   "   "   "
John McLean,................   "   "   "
W. B. Maclean,.............   "   "   "
Mrs. W. B. Maclean,.........   "   "   "
Wallace McLean,.............   "   "   "

Mrs. Wallace McLean, ... Toronto, Ont., Canada.
Miss Lucy Howard Maclean, ...   ''   ''   ''
Miss Maclean Howard, ...   ''   ''   '
Mrs. Maclean Davidson, ... Canada.
David McLean, ... Danbury, Conn.
Mrs. David McLean, ...   ''   ''
Mrs. Sallie P. McL. Greene, ... Simsbury,   ''
Mrs. Helen McL. Kimball, ... Washington, D. C.
Alexander McLean, Jr. . . . . 1320 Dunning Street, Chicago, Ill.
Arthnr A. Maclean, ... Monadnock Building,   ''   ''
Mrs. Arthur A. Maclean, . . .'. . . . Chicago, Ill.
Capt. Archibald B. McLean, ...   ''   ''
Mrs. Archibald B. McLean, ...   ''   ''
Archibald B. McLean, Jr., ... LaSalle Street, Chicago, Ill.
Mrs. Archibald B. McLean, Jr., .   ''   ''   ''   ''
A. O. McLain, ... Board Trade Building, Chicago, Ill.
Mrs. A. O. McLain, ...
Charles McLean, ...
Charles R. McLain, ... Board Trade Building, Chicago, Ill.
Mrs. Charles R. McLain, ...
Judge Eugene Carey, ... Chicago, Ill.
Donald MacLean, ... 489 So. Halstead St.,   ''   ''
James A. McLean, ... Chicago, Ill.
Mrs. James A. McLean, ...   ''   ''
James A. McLane, ... 100 Washington St., Chicago, Ill.
John L. McLean, ... 351 Rush Street,   ''   ''
John W. McLean, ... 44 State Street,   ''   ''
Mrs. John W. McLean, ... Chicago, Ill.
Peter MacLean, ...   ''   ''
Mrs. Peter MacLean, ...   ''   ''
Samuel A. McLean, Jr., ...   ''   ''
Mrs. Samuel A. McLean, Jr., . . .   ''   ''
Miss Viola McLean, ...   ''   ''
W. A. McLean, ... 4001 Grand Boulevard, Chicago, Ill.
Mrs. W. A. McLean, ... ''   ''   ''   ''   ''
Thomas A. Maclean, ... Monadnock Building,   ''   ''
Mrs. Thomas A. Maclean, ... Chicago, Ill.
Mrs. Wood McLean, ...   ''   ''
Mrs. Agnes McL. Foss, ...   ''   ''
———— Morse, ...   ''   ''

Mrs. Morse,...................Chicago, Ill.
H. Memory,............... ....   "   "
William Fraser,.............Elgin,   "
Dr. C. T. McLean,.............Hallsville, Ill.
Hon. Alexander McLean,.......Macomb,   "
B. F. McLean,................   "   "
Dr. John McLean,.............Pullman,   "
Mrs. John McLean,............   "   "
Guy McLean,.................   "   "
Miss Maud Cameron,...........   "   "
Archibald Maclean,............Rockford,   "
Mrs. Archibald Maclean,.......   "   "
Miss Helen Maclean,...........   "   "
William McLean,..............Tampico,   "
Dr. J. W. McLean,............Fayette, Iowa.
J. W. McLean,................College Springs, Iowa.
Mrs. J. W. McLean,...........   "   "   "
Lachlan McLean,..............Wichita, Kansas.
Thomas K. McLean,...........   "   "
Dr. Donald MacLean,..........Detroit, Mich.
Mrs. Donald MacLean,.........   "   "
Richard Earle MacLean,........Escanaba,   "
D. T. Macdonald,..............Red Jacket, Mich.
John T. McLean,..............Clarke, Neb.
Mrs. John T. McLean,.........   "   "
Daniel MacLean,..............Omaha,   "
Donald McLean,..............Louisiana, Missouri.
Dr. James Maxwell, ...Tobermory, Isle of Mull.
Dr. Thomas Neil McLean,......Elizabeth, N. J.
Rev. Calvin B. McLean,........Palmyra,   "
Mrs. Sarah McL. Abernethy,....30 West 56th St., New York, N. Y.
Hon. Donald McLean,..........170 Broadway,   "   "   "
Mrs. Donald McLean,..........   "   "   "   "
Mrs. Helen McL. Wotherspoon,.119 West 11th St.,   "   "   "
William W. Wotherspoon,......   "   "   "   "
Mrs. Harriet McL. Ammous,....Franklin, Ohio.
E. L. McClain, ...Greenfield,   "
Mrs. E. L. McClain, ...   "   "
John P. MacLean, ...Greenville,   "
Mrs. John P. MacLean, ...   "   "

Dr. J. T. Maclean,.............New Philadelphia.
Mrs. Eda W. Maclean, M. D., ..   "   "
Archibald McLean, ...Bradford, Pa.
Mrs. Archibald McLean, ...   "   "
William Arch. McClain,........Gettysburg, Pa.
Mrs. William Arch. McClain, ...   "   "
Miss Olivia C. McClain,.........   "   "
Mrs. H. W. Wilkinson, ...Providence, R. I.
Miss Anna Reed Wilkinson, ...   "   "
Hiram H. McLane, ...San Antonio, Texas.
Mrs. Hiram H. McLane, ...   "   "
Roderick M. McLean,..........Spokane Falls, Wash.
Dr. Thomas B. McLain, ...Wheeling, W. Va.
Mrs. Thomas B. McLain, ...   "   "
Colin C. McLean,..............Janesville, Wis.
Mrs. Colin C. McLean,.........   "   "
George C. McLean, ...   "   "
Mrs. George C. McLean,........   "   "
Dr. W. F. McLean,............Elyria, Ohio.
D. T. Macdonald,..............Calumet, Mich.
Malcolm MacLean, ...Ogalalla, Neb.
Dr. Donald McLean, ...Denver, Col.
Mrs. Donald McLean,..........   "   "

LIST OF OFFICERS AND MEMBERS

OF

CLAN MACLEAN ASSOCIATION.

PRESIDENT:

WILLIAM A. McLEAN, 4001 Grand Boulevard, Chicago, Ill.

TREASURERS:

ARTHUR A. MACLEAN, Monadnock Building, Chicago, Ill.
THOMAS A. MACLEAN, Monadnock Building, Chicago, Ill.

SECRETARIES:

S. P. MACLEAN, Tribune Building, Chicago, Ill.
ARTHUR A. MACLEAN, Monadnock Building, Chicago, Ill.

CORRESPONDING SECRETARY:

JOHN P. MACLEAN, Greenville, Ohio.

MEMBERS:

Agnes M. Maclean,............Berkeley, Cal.
J. O. Maclean,...............Los Angeles, Cal.
Rev. Dr. J. K. McLean,.......Oakland,   "
R. McKillicun,...............   "   "
Dr. Robert A. McLean,........San Francisco, Cal.
Major Hugh H. McLean,........St. John, N. B., Canada.
Hector MacLean,..............Bridgetown, N. S., Canada.
Rev. Archibald McLean,.......Blyth, Ont.,   "
W. H. McLean,................Crinan, "   "
D. J. McLain,................Fort Erie, Ont.,   "
Archibald McLean,............Glencoe, Ontario, Can.
Allan MacLean,...............Kingston, "   "
W. A. McLean,................Owen Sound, Ont., "
Capt. J. B. McLean,..........Toronto, Ont., Canada.
Frank W. McLean,............   "   "   "
G. D. McClain,...............Denver, Colo.

David McLean, ... Danbury, Conn.
Mrs. Helen McL. Kimball, ... Washington, D. C.
Lieut. Walter McLean, U. S. N.,   "   "
A. McLean, ... Chicago, Ill.
Angus A. Maclean, ...   "   "
Capt. Archibald B. McLean, ...   "   "
Archibald B. McLean, ... LaSalle Street, Chicago, Ill.
A. O. McLean, ... Board Trade Building, Chicago, Ill.
Charles R. McLain, ...   "   "   "
Charles Maclean, ... Chicago, Ill.
Donald MacLean, ... 489 So. Halstead St., Chicago, Ill.
Frank Maclean, ... Chicago, Ill.
James A. McLane, ... 100 Washington St., Chicago, Ill.
John W. McLean, ... 44 State Street, Chicago, Ill.
Rev. Lachlan Maclean, ... Chicago, Ill.
M. A. Maclean, ...   "   "
Peter Maclean, ... •   "
Samuel A. McLean, Jr., ...   "   "
W. H. McLean, ...   "   "
Mrs. Agnes McL. Foss, ...   "   "
John H. McKay, ...   "   "
William Fraser, ... Elgin,   "
John McLean, ... Grand Crossing, Ill.
Dr. C. T. McLean, ... Hallsville,   "
Alexander McLean, ... Joliet,   "
J. M. McLean, ... Kingston,   "
Hon. Alexander McLean, ... Macomb,   "
B. F. McLean, ...   "   "
Dr. John McLean, ... Pullman,   "
Guy McLean, ...   "   "
Louis A. McLean, ... Urbana,   "
J. L. McLean, ... Winnebago,   "
Prof. H. Z. McLain, ... Crawfordsville, Ind.
Mrs. Catharine McL. New, ... Indianapolis,   "
J. W. McLean, ... College Springs, Iowa.
S. V. Smith, ... Davenport,   "
Dr. J. W. McLean. . . . . Fayette,   "
Hon. Emlin McClain, ... Iowa City,   "
Lachlan McLean, ... Wichita, Kan.
Thomas K. McLean, ...   "   "

Carey McLain,..............Wellsville, Kansas.
George C. McClean,.... ......Springfield, Mass.
S. Adelbert McLean,..........Bay City, Mich.
Dr. Donald MacLean,..........Detroit,　"
Richard E. MacLean,..........Escanaba,　"
T. D. Macdonald, ...Red Jacket, Mich.
Dr. John McLean, ...Morehead, Minn.
William McLean,..............Albion, Nebraska.
John T. McLean, ...Clarke,　"
Malcolm Maclean, ...Ogalalla,　"
Daniel Maclean, ...Omaha,　"
Dr. Thomas Neil McLean,......Elizabeth, N. J.
Rev. Calvin B. McLean,........Palmyra,　"
Charles McLean, ...New York, N. Y.
Hon. Donald McLean, ...170 Broadway, New York. N. Y.
Mrs. Sarah McL. Abernethy, ...39 West 56 St., "　"　"
Mrs. Helen McL. Wotherspoon,.119 West 11th St., New York, N. Y.
Dr. W. F. McLean,...........Elyria, Ohio.
J. L. McLean,.................Massillon, Ohio.
C. M. Russell,................　"　"
Dr. J. T. Maclean,.............New Philadelphia, Ohio.
Elsmore T. King, ...Richwood,　"
William McLean,..............Toledo,　"
Archibald McLean, ...Bradford, Pa.
Judge William McClain, ...Gettysburg, Pa.
William Arch. McClain,........,　"　"
John McLean,.....-..........Philadelphia, Pa.
Hector McLean,..............Sugar Grove, "
John McLean,.................　"　"　"
Mrs. H. W. Wilkinson, ...Providence, R. I.
Joseph Maclean,..............Knoxville, Tenn.
Hiram H. McLane, ...San Antonio, Texas.
Martin McLean,..............Davenport, Washington.
Roderick McLean,............Spokane Falls,　"
Dr. Thomas B. McLain, ...Wheeling, West Va.
Colin C. McLean, ...Janesville, Wis.
George C. McLean, ...　"　"
William C. McLean, ...Menomonie, Wis.
Miss Sarah McLean, ...Milwaukee,　"